# Your Unique FIZEEK!

A Girl's Guide to Faith, Fuel, and
Finding Your Superpowers

**Dr. Tiffany Watson**

PUBLISHED BY StoryBuilders Press

Print ISBN: 978-1-954521-83-4

Digital ISBN: 978-1-954521-84-1

First Edition

# Dedication

*This book is for all the girls, the women who were once girls...*
*and the moms who are raising girls.*

*May you live a life of purpose and of passion. May you walk boldly*
*showing the world the gifts and beauty that live within each of us.*

*Find your footing, focus on Him, and never, ever give up.*

# **Access the Free Resources Mentioned in this Book:**

Check out Dr. Tiff's "Your Unique Fizeek Fuel Up Plan"

Listen to Megan Woods' song "The Truth"

Meet other Fizeek Girls and check out the Community in the Fizeek Girls! App

# Acknowledgements

*An endeavor such as writing a book, it takes your whole heart, it takes your fullest attention and your deepest emotion. Often the people in your life are impacted in some way. Hopefully for the better, but often it is a sacrifice of time, attention and emotional energy. This passion project, Fizeek, has asked that the people around me support, and love and cheer me on because this is such an important body of work. These things take a team, and what a team God has put around me.*

*Thank you, mom and dad, for always being my biggest cheerleaders. For pulling me up when I stumble, for dusting me off when my arms were too tired, and for pushing me down the narrow road when I wanted to take a detour.*

*To my Storybuilder's team, Sarah & Erin, and everyone else behind the scenes, you have been a blessing. The guidance, the support and enthusiasm for this book has kept me motivated and inspired to share my superpowers with the world.*

# Contents

# Chapter 1
# Hey, Girl!

Has anyone ever told you how awesome you are? I'm not just saying that. Seriously. Think about all the cool things that make you, well, *you*. The skills and gifts, the qualities that no one else can claim that God created especially for you.

Maybe you are a big sister or a little sister. Maybe you are an only child. Maybe you have crazy **curly hair** and bright blue eyes. Are you super flexible? Can you run faster than everyone in your class or jump really high? Do you **love to dance** or sing? Have a knack for remembering numbers? Can you spell long, hard words without writing them down? Have **you traveled** to lots of different countries and met all kinds of interesting people?

All the things about you that are different and interesting make you unique—as in *one of a kind*.

Think about snowflakes, stars, or leaves on a tree. They are all just a little bit different. I know sometimes when people say you are "different," you think it means you are "weird." Maybe it does. But being weird is not always bad. You don't know me that well yet, but I would say I am a weirdo, and being different is *not* a bad thing. Girl, I would rather be different, unique, and ME than the same as everyone else. I would rather own my unique Fizeek and use the gifts God gave me than to hide my light away from the world.

Oh, what is *Fizeek*? I'm so glad you asked.

Well, it's not a real word! I made it up. There is a real word called **physique**, which is pronounced just like my word *Fizeek*. But my word is *so* much better.

> **physique:** the form, size, and development of a person's body.

*Physique* is limited to talking about our looks, our outside appearance. But *Fizeek* is about your unique mind, body, and character. It covers everything from the inside out—which, IMHO, is way more important to build than just your physique.

How do I know? Because there is a great Bible verse that confirms that we are created exactly on purpose. And what could be more cool and important than that?

*¹³ For it was you who created my inward parts; you knit me together in my mother's womb.*

*¹⁴ I will praise you because I have been remarkably and wondrously made. Your works are wondrous, and I know this very well.*

Psalm 139:13–14

All those cool things we talked about before from your talents and abilities to the activities that you love and do well—all of them make up your Fizeek. It could even include things that you don't do that well yet but are working on. It starts with your personality (like your sense of humor, intelligence, and creativity) and your core values (like kindness, honesty, generosity, and your beliefs).

But Fizeek also means the color of your skin, hair, and eyes or how tall (or short) you are. If you were made curvy or just straight up and down. Whether you have little feet or big ones.

And Fizeek includes the things we do, how well we listen and connect with other people, how we treat other people. All those qualities are important in making us the absolute best and coolest version of ourselves. When we own our actions and behaviors, then others get to be *unique* too! That's a *win-win* in my book (and this book too).

But before you start listening to me, I bet you want to know who I am.

**Hi! I'm Dr. Tiff,** but I usually don't call myself that! I have been Tipp, Tipp-a-canoe (don't ask), Tiff, Tiffany, T. Dubs, Coach Tiff. I have been called a lot of things in my forty-four years of life. Yep, I am forty-four, and I have a sweet cocker spaniel named Tucker. Tiff and Tucker. Cute, huh?

Before I was Dr. Tiff—before I worked with girls and women, and before I worked with people of all ages and backgrounds—I was a baby girl, a teenager, a little sister, a daughter, a friend, an athlete, a word nerd, and sometimes an honor student. If you are going through it, thinking about it, dealing with it, wondering about it, trying it, I have probably either experienced it, or know someone who has.

Growing up, I faced *all the things*: boys, puberty, annoying parents and teachers. I fought with my older brother, but then sometimes we were best buddies. I went to school dances. I permed my hair. (If you don't know what that is, ask your mom. But definitely *do not* try it. Bad decision.) I also played soccer and basketball from kindergarten through high school. **I was really good at soccer** and had the chance to play in college. I was in a few plays during school. Never the lead role. I cannot carry a tune, and I have no rhythm.

I have coached middle school and high school soccer, basketball, and softball. I taught at a college for four years and published books. One year I recorded a new podcast episode every week. It was super fun—and hard! I am very creative but not an artist. I know my superpowers (something we will talk about soon!), and I am always willing to try finding new ones.

I went through some tough stuff too. Phases where I hated shopping for clothes. My body was stubborn sometimes, not always looking or functioning like I wanted it to. I had pimples and awkwardness. But then there were years where I was totally fine with how I looked and felt. I loved my hair, and my skin was clear. All these phases have been a super-fun, scary, tiring, confusing, but exhilarating roller-coaster ride that landed me where I am now.

The coolest part about my life today is I get to chat with, learn about, **support, coach, and work alongside girls** just like I used to be and maybe like you are right now. You're on the verge of the next new, big thing in your life, and it's hard.

It's hard to understand who we are, who we want to become, and how to navigate the world whenever everything about our lives is changing all at once. So think of this book as a guide to help you through the hard parts, or rather, it's your training manual to help you build your Fizeek, with me as your coach.

Don't worry! This isn't gym class. I'm not going to make you run laps around your house or anything. But I want to offer some helpful advice and more Bible verses that have guided me and others.

The rest of the book is broken into three parts to help train your Fizeek, where each chapter explores a specific part of your Fizeek, shares an entry from the *"Diary of a Real Girl,"* and challenges you to an activity called *"Chapter Challenge,"* where you can have a chance to put each chapter into practice.

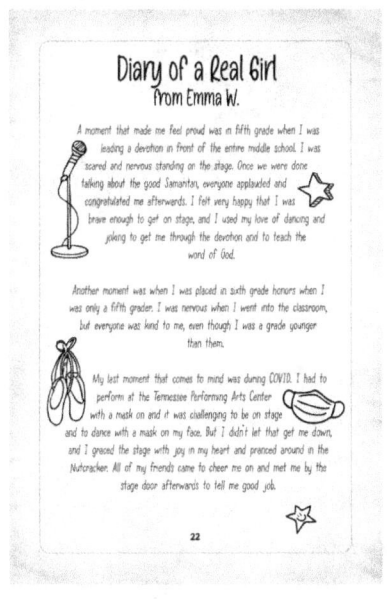

### Chapter Challenge 1:
#### Identify Personal Strengths and Traits

Both Bella and Emma were scared to share their gifts with others, but once they did, they felt great and understood how much joy they could bring to others by being uniquely themselves. Now it's your turn to find the things that make you uniquely you.

Grab your favorite notebook, write in the margins of this book, or take electronic notes, and follow the prompts below. Hold on to your answers as well be looking back at them throughout the rest of the book. It feels good to read about and remember how special you are on days when you're feeling less than. On days like that, you might even write your superpowers down on a sticky note (or several) and post it in your bathroom, bedroom, or wherever you want, so that all day long, you see reminders about how awesome you are.

#### What Makes Me Unique?
Write down five things that make you different from your friends or classmates. These can be skills, hobbies, or personality traits.

#### My Proud Moments
Reflect on three moments in your life when you felt proud of yourself. What did you do, and what strengths did you use?

#### Compliment Collection
List five compliments you've received from others. How do they make you feel? What strengths do they highlight about you?

#### My Superpowers
Imagine you have superpowers based on your strengths. What would they be? Describe how you would use them to help others.

**"Part One: Finding Your Superpowers"** is all about your character because that's where everything about you begins. We'll explore your gifts (I like to call them superpowers), your core values and beliefs, and how important they all are and how to use them in the world.

**"Part Two: Fueling Your Superpowers"** covers your physical body—how to feed it, move it, and care for it so that you're the strongest, healthiest you can be. After all, superheroes need a good breakfast before they go save the world!

**"Part Three: Sharing Your Superpowers"** is about being authentically, unapologetically you. It can be scary to share your gifts with others. But by tapping into the core of who you are and relying on God who dwells in you, you have nothing to fear. So walk boldly, with your head held high, and be the person God created you to be!

Are you ready to get started? If so, hold on to your seat, girl, because this is going to be quite a ride. There will be ups and downs, aha moments, and exciting discoveries! The best part is that God and I will be walking right alongside you the whole time. While you are reading, learning, and practicing, there are other girls out there doing the very same thing—discovering their unique Fizeek and learning how to *stand up*, *step up*, and *show up* in a big way, every day.

**Just a note:** Throughout the book, you may find some topics that you'll want to talk through more with someone you trust. I would love to just tell you, *"Hey! Go talk to your mom or dad!"* But let's be real here: that probably won't happen. (If you do have that type of relationship, that is *amazing*—totally lean into it!) Try to find an adult you can talk to. This could be a coach, a teacher, a youth group leader, maybe an aunt or uncle, or even a best friend's parent. Whoever it is, there is nothing quite like having an adult on your side, ready to listen and give advice (if you want it, that is!).

I hope you love all the opportunities I've included throughout the chapters to explore additional materials, resources, and challenges. I would absolutely love to hear from you, so please reach out to me if you have questions! I hope you love reading this as much as I have loved writing it. *Let's do this!*

Meet other Fizeek Girls and check out the Community in the Fizeek Girls! App

# Part One

*Finding Your Superpowers*

# Chapter 2

# You Are Made Uniquely *YOU*

*¹³ I can do all things through Christ who gives me strength.*

*Philippians 4:13*

**Meet Bella.** She's a lot like you . . .

Bella Harrison had always felt like an ordinary seventh grader. At thirteen, she was still trying to pinpoint what made her special. Her school was full of students who all seemed to have their talents all figured out. There was Tanya, the math whiz who always aced every test. Jordan, the fastest sprinter in the whole school, never failed to amaze during gym class. And then there was Bella, who often felt lost in the crowd.

"What is *my* strength?" she would ask God in her daily prayers. "When do I get to find out my gifts?"

One afternoon during her English class, something changed. Bella's teacher, Mrs. Emory, announced that they would be writing short stories for the school's literary magazine.

"Writing allows us to express our superpowers with words," Mrs. Emory explained.

Bella was skeptical. What could she possibly write about?

*You have to have a superpower before you can use it*, she thought to herself. *Ugh*.

That night Bella sat at her desk staring at a blank laptop screen. Her puppy, Tucker, lay at her feet. He was her best buddy.

Before she began writing, **Bella folded her hands and prayed,** "God, please help me find the words."

Suddenly, she felt a sense of inspiration and clarity. She began writing a story about a girl who could talk to animals. The words flowed so easily, almost as if someone had opened a soda and all the fizz just started bubbling out. By the time she finished, she felt something she hadn't before: she felt proud of herself.

A week after Bella turned in her story, Mrs. Emory pulled her aside.

"Bella, this is extraordinary," she said. "You have a gift for storytelling. Have you considered joining the Creative Writing Club?"

Bella's face lit up. Maybe, just maybe, writing was her superpower. Maybe that is how God made her unique.

# What It Means to Be Unique

According to this old guy named **Webster** (if you're like me and have a crazy imagination, I'm picturing a mix of Santa Claus and Dumbledore from Harry Potter; if you aren't a Harry Potter fan, think long, white beard; wise, knowing smile; glasses; and someone who probably loves cookies), *uniqueness* means, "the quality of being particularly remarkable, special, or unusual." Two words stand out to me here: *remarkable* and *unusual*.

**Remarkable**—that sounds like a compliment to me. Re-*mark*-able, meaning you are leaving a lasting *mark* on the people you meet, even if you don't know it. It could be a silent, unintentional mark, like a smile at the checkout line, a "Good job!" shout-out to one of your teammates, or being on time and attentive in class. Not everyone makes an effort to do those things, so when you do, people remember.

> **remarkable:** worthy of attention; striking

To me, being remarkable has nothing to do with accomplishments, trophies, awards, or skills. But we can all be remarkable by making others feel important. Think about times when someone went out of their way to make you feel special or seen. They didn't have to show off their skills or achieve some amazing feat in order to make you feel that way, did they? It could have just been a simple, everyday act.

So imagine if you did those little things every day for someone you care about? Then you would be remarkable in their eyes too!

**Unusual**—look at what's right in the middle of that word: *you!* Un-*you*-sual. Like *weird*, the word *unusual* tends to take on a negative connotation or meaning. But think of things like artwork with unique colors or abstract shapes, birds that have really crazy feathers, or foods that have a funky texture but that taste so yummy. They are unusual, maybe even weird, but man, they are cool and interesting!

> **unusual:** remarkable or interesting because different from or better than others

*Unusual* can also mean that you have a different way of seeing the world. No one else has the same magnifying glass to see things as you do, picks up on the same details, or understands things in the exact same way as you. Your lens might highlight certain parts of a situation, while someone else is looking through binoculars or a telescope. They are seeing a different angle of the same scene. But neither of them is wrong, right?

Uniqueness might also be about your family tree or the history of your name, where you were born, or where your parents grew up. All those experiences and all the history create memories that change how we walk through this world. Maybe this is about the types of foods you eat at Thanksgiving and Christmas or where you choose to worship or pray. Every family has its own unique traditions that contribute to who we are.

Here are some of my favorite traditions:

**My family eats chili on Halloween.** Even if it is seventy degrees in October, we still eat it. And my dad likes his chili with a burnt hot dog—I'm talkin' cooked-over-the-fire, dark, shriveled hot dog. Gross.

When I was in middle school, we would take a road trip to Atlanta every summer to pick out new clothes for the first day of school. Along the way, we stopped at Dairy Queen for a Blizzard. Butterfinger is still my favorite.

**My older brother and I swap our Christmas presents on Christmas Eve** instead of Christmas Day so we always get to start the holiday early!

This is all to say that sometimes we don't always know what makes us unique. We don't always see our uniqueness as something special, but it really is. God made you unique for a specific purpose. So instead of viewing your uniqueness as a weakness or a curse, let's learn to love it as the gift it is.

# Diary of a Real Girl
## from Emma W.

A moment that made me feel proud was in fifth grade when I was leading a devotion in front of the entire middle school. I was scared and nervous standing on the stage. Once we were done talking about t h e good Samaritan, everyone applauded and congratulated me afterwards. I felt very happy that I was brave enough to get on stage, and I used my love of dancing and joking to get me through the devotion and to teach the word of God.

Another moment was when I was placed in sixth grade honors when I was only a fifth grader. I was nervous when I went into the classroom, but everyone was kind to me, even though I was a grade younger than them.

My last moment that comes to mind was during COVID. I had to perform at the Tennessee Performing Arts Center with a mask on and it was challenging to be on stage and to dance with a mask on my face. But I didn't let that get me down, and I graced the stage with joy in my heart and pranced around in the Nutcracker. All of my friends came to cheer me on and met me by the stage door afterwards to tell me good job.

# Chapter Challenge 1:
## Identify Personal Strengths and Traits

Both Bella and Emma were scared to share their gifts with others, but once they did, they felt great and understood how much joy they could bring to others by being uniquely themselves. Now it's your turn to find the things that make you uniquely you.

Grab your favorite notebook, write in the margins of this book, or take electronic notes, and follow the prompts below. Hold on to your answers as we'll be looking back at them throughout the rest of the book. It feels good to read about and remember how special you are on days when you're feeling less than. On days like that, you might even write your superpowers down on a sticky note (or several) and post it in your bathroom, bedroom, or wherever you want, so that all day long, you see reminders about how awesome you are.

## What Makes Me Unique?
Write down five things that make you different from your friends or classmates. These can be skills, hobbies, or personality traits.

## My Proud Moments
Reflect on three moments in your life when you felt proud of yourself. What did you do, and what strengths did you use?

## Compliment Collection
List five compliments you've received from others. How do they make you feel? What strengths do they highlight about you?

## My Superpowers
Imagine you have superpowers based on your strengths. What would they be? Describe how you would use them to help others.

# Some Real Fizeek Girl Responses:

I am charismatic.

I am a good friend.

I can run really fast and jump pretty high too.

I love to sing and dance.

I am a really good at braiding hair.

My little sister loves hanging out with me.

I can make graphics and cool digital images.

This is a short list of super powerful gifts that some of my real Fizeek girls submitted when I asked them what they thought their superpowers were. You might have these same talents and skills or a whole list of other ones. There is no right answer. And no one else has to agree with you either.

That's the coolest part of our unique Fizeek: we *own* it. If we see something in ourselves, it is the truth. Now, sometimes we might see it and not share it as much as we could. When that happens, no one is able to benefit from our superpowers. If you know anything about superpowers, you know that we are given those gifts so that we can help others! It is our responsibility to make an impact using our gifts as often as we can. Sharing our superpowers also gives others the confidence to use their gifts. Then, all of a sudden, we are helping and changing many more people together.

Some of our gifts we can use every day, like being a good friend—that is a superpower that you can practice several times a day. But something like **making art** or **braiding hair** might be something that comes in handy in very specific situations, such as getting ready for a game or a presentation. When I think about my own superpowers, one of them is being able to put all these words on paper to help you show up, step up, and stand up into your purpose!

The gifts that God has given us are always there; we just have to make sure we are looking for them and ready to use them when the opportunity comes around. It is so easy to ignore them or not even realize they exist. But here's the thing: we usually get clues along the way. This is where you can plug into your superpower potential.

# Chapter Challenge 2:
## Find Your Spark Plug

In the graphic below, you can see a little spark plug in the middle of the circles. This is your sweet spot, where everything comes together and your superpowers live. To figure out where your sweet spot might be, think about three things:

1) What you love to do
2) What you are good at doing
3) What you can make the biggest impact doing

The activities, skills, or values that can answer all three of these questions is one of your superpower sweet spots. There might be more than one too!

## Discovering Your Superpower

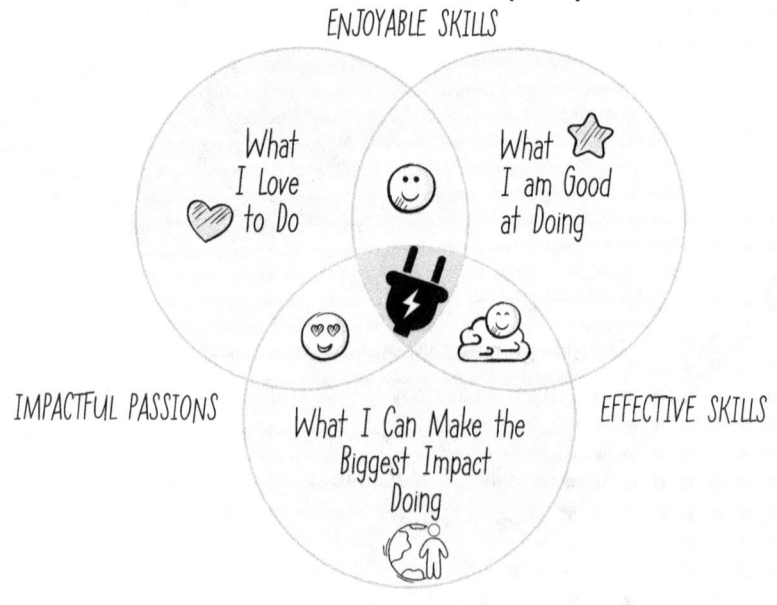

ENJOYABLE SKILLS

What I Love to Do

What I am Good at Doing

IMPACTFUL PASSIONS

EFFECTIVE SKILLS

What I Can Make the Biggest Impact Doing

# Here's mine:

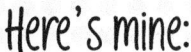

WHAT I LOVE DOING

Playing Sports and Being Active

Playing Sports and Overcoming Physical Challenges

WHAT I CAN MAKE AN IMPACT DOING

Helping People Fall in Love with Being Active and Taking Care of their Health

WHAT I'M GOOD AT DOING

Looking at my answers, this means two of my superpower sweet spots are coaching sports and helping people improve their health. See how there is a sweet spot where the things we love, the things we do well, and the things that can make an impact on others all come together? When you plug into that superpower, you can set the world on fire.

## Let's try another example:

**What I love doing:**
hanging out with friends

**What I am good at doing:**
being social and thinking of fun things to do with friends

**What I could make the biggest impact doing:**
connecting people who share interests in the same activities and passions

One of your superpower sweet spots could be building communities or bringing groups of people together for support and connection. This might be starting an after-school study group or forming a book club or a group that gets together on Saturdays to play video games.

Take some time to think about the things you love, the things you are good at, and how you could use these to make a lasting, remarkable impact on others and, in the process, bring yourself joy and fulfillment as well. That is one way you find your superpowers.

Chapter 3

# Unveiling Your Superpowers

Despite her newfound confidence in writing, Bella still struggled with self-doubt. **One weekend she and her mom went on a hike to a nearby nature reserve.**

"You've been working so hard," her mom said. "Sometimes it helps to slow down and think about what really matters to you."

As they climbed the trail, Bella thought about what was important to her, deep in her core. She loved storytelling, but why? Was it because she liked the attention?

No, she realized, it was because stories had the power to make people feel seen and understood. Stories were the great equalizer.

At the end of the hike, her mom handed her a notebook and asked, "If you could write a letter to your future self, what would it say?"

Bella sat on a rock and prayed silently.

*God, help me understand what's really important to me*, she thought.

Then she wrote: "Dear Future Me, always remember that your words can make a difference. Stay kind, stay curious, and never stop dreaming."

By the time they got back to the car, Bella felt more grounded in who she was and what she stood for—kindness, learning, and chasing the things that you believe in.

# The Heart of Your Fizeek

How we show up in the world is deeply rooted in two things: our beliefs and our core values. These are intimately connected, but they have different roles in helping us to define who we are and what we stand for. We form beliefs based on experiences and education. Beliefs are kind of like opinions; only it is very hard to change our mind about our beliefs once we have developed them. Beliefs form our perceptions of ourselves, others, and the world. Think religion or politics, how we define a healthy relationship or the types of behaviors we "believe" are appropriate in school, church, or other people's homes. Beliefs are the lenses we use to see the world. They often help us choose our core **values**. But more specifically, our beliefs determine how we express those values.

> **values:** a person's principles or standards of behavior; one's judgment of what is important in life

As we start to develop opinions and make choices in life, our **beliefs** help us to establish what we call our core values. Our core is our center.

> **beliefs:** trust, faith, or confidence in someone or something

When we think about the *center* of things, what purpose does it serve?

- The center of the circle?
- The center of attention?
- The center of the family?
- The center on a basketball team?
- Center stage?

In these examples, the center is often the most important—or at least a very significant—part of the structure or situation. We can all identify who the center, the rock, of our family is. Maybe a grandpa, an aunt, or maybe your mom or dad. Center stage is often where the spotlight is and where we strive to be in dance or theater. Many times the center of the circle is where the important information is stored. So in this case, our *core* is our center. It is where we find our most important beliefs and principles.

Your core values are the most essential, deepest layer of your Fizeek, the foundation. The verse in Galatians about the fruit of the Spirit lists several examples of core values, and they're a great place to start while you explore what yours might be. **Here are a few more core values:**

✔ Honesty
✔ Integrity
✔ Kindness
✔ Fairness
✔ Tolerance
✔ Respect
✔ Compassion

There are many more, but these are some of the most common and universal values. The reason they're so important is that our core values guide our choices. They help us make decisions, like who we choose to spend time with, when to say no, and when to jump in feet first. They might also direct us toward the types of activities we participate in.

For example, respect is what I would call one of the more universal core values. In nearly every culture, every class of society, at every age, and in every situation, people believe it is appropriate and of good character to show respect to our leaders, our elders, and our peers. However, the way we display that respect can vary drastically from culture to culture or situation to situation.

This is where beliefs come in. While we all agree respect is a core value, our beliefs about how respect is shown may be different. In many countries, it is respectful to bow or kneel in the presence of authority. Think **kings and queens, the pope, or spiritual leaders**. In the United States, however, we do not bow to our president or the pastor

of our church. Instead, we might stand when they enter the room or shake their hand. Another way we show respect is to say, "Yes, sir/ma'am," or "Yes, please," to our teachers and parents. We also might hold open the door for an older person as they go into the grocery store behind us.

Our core value of respect is a result of our *belief* that our elected and appointed leaders have earned certain courtesies and behaviors from others. But you can see how, depending on where we live or what/whom we look up to, those behaviors of respect may vary.

Understanding core values can also help you accept yourself for who you are and not feel pressured to try to be someone else. Likewise, they can help us accept others for who they are.

There's a saying, "Put yourself in their shoes." Remember the magnifying glass from chapter 2? How do we all have a unique way of looking at the world? Well, **"putting yourself in someone else's shoes"** means just that: if we want others to accept us and what we believe, then we need to reverse the situation and view it from the perspective of the other person to help us understand where they're coming from. This will help them feel heard and valued. We might not agree with what they believe or the choice they make, but we can still respect that the decision is theirs.

Further, our beliefs and core values play a significant role in sharpening and strengthening our superpowers. Think back to the last chapter and the superpower sweet spot, the spark plug graphic. The three questions we asked were, "What do you love?" "What are you good at?" and "What will make an impact?" The more aligned your passions are with your core values, the more natural it will feel as you work on strengthening them.

Think about something you love doing now, maybe **playing the piano or the guitar.** Your core value of discipline aligns with your passion to play and improve, which makes it easy to sit down and practice. On the other hand, when it comes to your chores, something you may not really love (who does?!), your value of discipline is a lot harder to stick with, isn't it?

I mean, you don't want this awesome outer shell that doesn't have anything inside, do you? It would be like getting the most

beautifully wrapped birthday present—glitter paper with big stars and hearts all over it. A shimmery, fancy, curly ribbon. A personalized, handwritten tag and card. But then when you rip open the box, it is empty. What a downer. Filling up your inner Fizeek has to come first because all of you begins in that deep strong core.

# Diary of a Real Girl
## from Sklyer R.

One time last year my dance studio shut down because of a dishonest incident, and I had nowhere to go. It was a really hard decision because there were so many different dance studios I could go to. I had to use my core value of honesty and faith in God to find a good path by thinking to myself what would be best for me and my love for dance.

I talked to many of my dance friends about where they would go, but I really wanted to dance, so it didn't matter if my friends chose the same dance studio I did. Eventually I prayed and thought to myself about where I should go and what was best for me. Sure enough, after the switch to a new studio, it turned out that most of my friends ended up there too. I love it there so much. I definitely made the right decision because I am thriving and loving dance so much. This is how I used my core values of honesty and faith.

# Chapter Challenge 1:
## Determine Personal Core Values

Read the list below, and write down or circle/highlight any of the words that jump out to you or any word that resonates with how you think of yourself or who you want to be.

| | |
|---|---|
| **Integrity** | being honest, transparent, and ethical |
| **Respect** | showing consideration and honoring others |
| **Compassion** | caring and empathizing with others' feelings and experiences |
| **Accountability** | taking responsibility for ones actions |
| **Creativity** | valuing imagination, innovation, and original thinking |
| **Kindness** | acting with warmth, care, and consideration toward others |
| **Gratitude** | appreciating what one has and expressing thanks |
| **Perseverance** | showing determination and resilience in the face of challenges |
| **Growth** | embracing personal and professional development |
| **Courage** | being brave in the face of fear or uncertainty |
| **Wisdom** | valuing knowledge, insight, and sound judgment |
| **Empathy** | understanding and sharing others' feelings and perspectives |
| **Fairness** | treating everyone justly and equally |
| **Loyalty** | being faithful and supportive to people or causes |
| **Teamwork** | valuing collaboration and working effectively with others |
| **Authenticity** | being true to oneself and honest with others |
| **Generosity** | giving freely and with an open heart |
| **Optimism** | looking on the bright side and expecting good outcomes |
| **Justice** | advocating for what is fair and right |
| **Discipline** | demonstrating self-control and commitment to goals |
| **Humility** | having a modest view of ones importance |
| **Patience** | being tolerant and able to wait calmly |
| **Responsibility** | being reliable and dependable in actions and words |
| **Service** | putting others' needs before ones own; helping those in need |
| **Curiosity** | being open to learning and exploring new ideas |
| **Balance** | prioritizing a healthy balance among different aspects of life |
| **Independence** | valuing freedom, self-reliance, and autonomy |
| **Tolerance** | accepting and embracing diversity in people and opinions |
| **Joy** | valuing happiness, fun, and a positive outlook on life |
| **Forgiveness** | letting go of grudges and resentment toward others |
| **Diligence** | putting in consistent effort and hard work |
| **Honesty** | valuing truth and sincerity in words and actions |
| **Self-respect** | holding oneself in high regard and setting boundaries |
| **Health** | prioritizing physical and mental well-being |
| **Flexibility** | being adaptable and open to change |

As we talked about earlier, your beliefs and core values help you make decisions all the time. So right now, let's spend ten to fifteen minutes thinking about why you chose those words. Think about the following questions:

- Does the word describe you?
- Do you wish the word described you (and maybe this is something you can work on)?
- Is the word a trait you see and admire in another person?
- Do you think you *should* want that word to describe you because of pressure from other people?
- If you think you *should* want something, where does that *should* come from? Yourself? Or someone else?
- When you say each word, how does that make your body feel?
- Are there any physical responses or sensations to specific words?

For example, *tolerance* makes me feel open and free, like a big hug. *Responsibility* makes me feel a little heavy and weighed down. Reflecting on your chosen core values makes them stronger because you know the why, the reason behind the choice. And the why helps us stand solid when confusion or doubt clouds our judgment. When faced with several options, you can think ahead and consider how certain choices may not have one right answer, but using our core values as our guide, we can find the right choice for us.

# Chapter Challenge 2:
## Determine Personal Core Values

We've spent a lot of time talking about core values and beliefs and picking specific words to describe them. Let's put them all together now into your personal mission statement.

You may have seen a business mission statement, or maybe your school, church, or club has a mission statement. Mission statements essentially describe what someone wants to achieve and how they'll do it using their core values. They're used to guide decisions to help a person or organization stay true to their core values, especially when the choice might be hard or scary. For example, if you value learning and growth, one of your mission statements might be, "I will seek opportunities where I can learn and grow." In action, this mission statement will then help you choose classes or activities because you'll look for the subjects or activities that will challenge you to learn something new or grow in some way—like choosing to move up to the next math class or taking on a leadership role in your youth group.

> I WILL ACT WITH COMPASSION AND KINDNESS, EVEN WHEN IT'S HARD.

> I WILL JOYOUSLY SERVE OTHERS SO THAT GOD'S LOVE MAY FLOW THROUGH ME ONTO THEM.

Now it's your turn. Using the words you circled in your reflection from "Chapter Challenge 1," practice writing "I will . . ." statements that explain what you want to do and how you will do it. In the example above, you want to learn and grow, so you will seek out opportunities that will help you learn and grow. Other personal mission statements might be, "I will act with compassion and kindness, even when it's hard," or "I will joyously serve others so that God's love may flow through me onto them."

**mission statement:** a formal summary of the aims and values of a company, organization, or individual.

# Chapter 4

# Using Your Gifts

> [10] *Each of you should use whatever gift you have received to serve others, as faithful stewards of God's grace in its various forms.*
>
> 1 Peter 4:10–11

Joining the Creative Writing Club was a social game-changer for Bella. The club met every Wednesday after school, and she quickly connected with other students who shared her passion. **There was Elena, who wrote poetry, and Max, who dreamed up out of this world sci-fi adventures.**

The club's first big project was to write and perform a short play for the school's talent showcase. **Bella's heart raced when she was asked to write the script.** She spent hours crafting a story about a

group of kids who discovered a magical treehouse. When the club read her script out loud, Bella couldn't believe the applause she received.

On the night of the showcase, Bella stood backstage, her hands shaking uncontrollably as she watched her friends bring her story to life. The audience laughed, gasped, and cheered in all the right places. Before stepping out to take a bow, Bella closed her eyes and thanked God for giving her the courage and creativity to share her talent.

By the end of the performance, Bella realized something important: her talent wasn't just about writing; it was about inspiring people and bringing them together through her words.

# Let Your Light Shine

In chapters 2 and 3, you identified the gifts that God has given you to make a difference in our world, and you understand the core values and beliefs guiding how you make decisions. Now we need to find the best and most impactful ways to put our gifts to work. The same superpowers can be super important in all different places and all different ways.

Maybe you learned that your gifts are compassion and humor and that you are a loyal friend and a good listener. Putting it all together, that may lead you to use your gifts to help those you love when they're having a tough time, like **sitting with a friend who's hurting** and allowing them to share their story with you. Or it could be **telling a joke** to brighten someone's day. Either way, you are sharing your gifts with others in a way only you can. And every time you share your gifts, they grow stronger, and God's love shines brighter through you.

Because here's the thing: they are not *our* gifts anyway; they are God's gifts that He gave to us to use. So if we don't get to work using them, He is going to keep nudging us and redirecting us until we do. So we might as well just put them out there, don't you think?

Think about the example of being tall. **You might choose to be a basketball or volleyball player or even just reach things on the top shelf at the grocery store for others!** (And if that's the case, I might just ask you to come shopping with me because I always have to get one of those step ladders when I can't reach something!) There's always more than one way to use your gifts.

Here's a list of other ways you can sharpen your superpowers. Check out the appendices for specific ideas for each.

**STEM (Science, Technology, Engineering, and Math) Activities**

- Coding and robotics
- Science experiments
- Engineering challenges

**Performing Arts**

- Drama and theater
- Dance
- Music lessons

**Sports and Physical Activities**

- Team sports
- Individual sports
- Yoga and mindfulness

**Writing and Storytelling**

- Creative writing
- Poetry
- Book clubs

**Entrepreneurship**

- Starting a small business
- DIY fundraisers

**Cultural Exploration**

- Language learning
- Exploring different cultures

**Creative Arts and Craft**

- Painting and drawing
- Craft projects
- Photography
- DIY projects

**Community Service and Leadership**

- Volunteering
- Girl Scouts or leadership clubs

**Outdoor Adventures**

- Hiking and nature exploration
- Camping and stargazing

**Culinary Arts**

- Baking and cooking
- Culinary classes

**Tech-Free and Relaxing Hobbies**

- Board Games and puzzles
- Mindfulness activities

**Gardening and Nature Projects**

- Starting a garden
- Sustainable living projects

It may not always be clear how you can best use your gifts, especially when you're still exploring what your gifts are. So don't be discouraged if it takes some time to find the path God set for you. Just look at the incredible women below. They didn't know what was in their future, but they kept using their superpowers and sharpening their skills, and they left a lasting impact on the world.

## Marie Curie

**Superpowers:** Scientific curiosity and innovation

**Inspiration:** Born in 1867 at a time when women were often discouraged from going to college or pursuing careers, she became the first woman to win a Nobel Prize and the only person to win in two different scientific fields (physics and chemistry). Marie Curie's work in radioactivity opened new doors in science. Her accomplishments encourage girls to pursue STEM careers and follow their passions in science.

## Jennifer Lopez

**Superpowers:** Acting and dancing

**Inspiration:** Capitalizing on her fame as an actress, singer, and dancer, JLo uses her spotlight to call attention to many social justice issues close to her heart. JLo and her sisters started the Lopez Family Foundation in 2009 to help deliver accessible, quality health care to mothers and their children, regardless of their ability to pay for care. In addition, JLo has solidified her reputation as a famous feminist through her work with Amnesty International. After learning about the high rate of femicide in Mexico, she teamed up with the organization to launch an awareness-raising bilingual website. JLo also produced and starred in the film *Borderland*, dedicated to exposing the ongoing murders of women activists in Juarez, Mexico. In 2015, the UN Foundation named Lopez a Global Advocate for Girls and Women. Her work inspires people to keep fighting for what's right, even when it's hard and seems impossible to change.

# Diary of a Real Girl
## from Sophia B.

I would like to think I have many superpowers. But one of my strongest is my ability to read a room. By this I mean I'm able to see if someone is looking upset or sad or even left out. I am able to see if one of my friends is going through a hard time, and this helps me be there for them and build them up.

God has given me a sense of compassion as well, for my friends or other people in my life. By having compassion, I am able to connect with people more, help them, and be reliable for them.

SUPER!!!  AWESOME!!  YEP!  HOW ARE YOU ?

One of my strongest gifts is being social. You may be asking yourself how being social is a gift? Well, let me tell you. Being social helps you get to know more people and make more friends. And get out there more. I can use this gift to connect to my friends that I make to God. For example, I invited some of my friends who have never been to church before to my youth group. I was able to give them an opportunity to get to experience God for the first time. You can use this specific gift in many other ways. That is just one specific way I use that gift.

Another gift I have is kindness. Now that may sound like something very simple or basic, but I can use this gift by being a light to others and showing them Jesus through me, which can be very hard to find sometimes in middle school; it can be even harder if you go to public school. But even in a dark place, I'm still able to spread the light and love of Jesus. I feel that God has given me many wonderful gifts, and I'm very blessed to have them.

I'd like to think that everyone has received a gift from God, but not everybody has discovered them yet. I most likely have more gifts of God and will discover more of them as I get older, and I think each gift is just as important.

# Diary of a Real Girl
## from Hanna T.

One time in my eighth grade class, there was a girl who tried to harm herself. I didn't know what it was like to feel so terrible about yourself to want to end it all. But when that happened, it deeply moved my heart, and I wrote her a song. It was a powerful connection, and I wanted to see her heart stop hurting. She eventually found her way.

Most people might not consider this a superpower, but I like writing in my journal. At first, I would just write about my day, but after I started the habit of writing and had been writing for many years, I realized that my writing became more for other people than just myself. I started writing poetry and stories and songs. The words that came out encouraged people that were going through tough times, and sometimes my songs talked about God and His beautiful creation! The more I wrote, the more I wanted to. The more I wanted to, the more people wanted to hear.

# Chapter Challenge 1:
## Share Your Gifts

I hope that this chapter has inspired you to use your superpowers and make a lasting impact on this world. With that in mind, pull your notebook out again. We're going to make a plan.

How I Use My Gifts

Thinking about your gifts and core values, write down the ways in which you are currently using your gifts, if you are. If you're not, think about what is holding you back and write that down too. Is it fear? Lack of opportunity? Something else? Maybe you're just not sure what to do? If you can pinpoint what's holding you back, then you'll know what you need to overcome in order to share your gifts.

Oftentimes the lesson comes through the struggle. And while God gave us gifts, He didn't guarantee that everything would come easy. But you can do all things through Him that gives you strength. After all, Marie and JLo all had things in their lives that they had to overcome. You can do it too.

Next, look back at the list on sharpening your superpowers. Does anything stand out to you? Are there any activities that you might like to try to do to grow and nurture your gifts? If so, write them down. What about those particular activities appeal to you? What do you like about them? If you're not sure yet, that's okay. Understanding the answers to those questions might one day help you decide what career you might choose to share your gifts in even bigger and better ways.

# Chapter Challenge 2:
## Sharpen Your Superpowers

As your coach, it's my job to help you grow. So over the next month, find and use or sharpen your superpowers in two to five new ways. After each, write a short reflection that talks about

(1) what you did,
(2) how you felt beforehand,
(3) how you felt after,
(4) and the result.

- Was this experience what you thought it was going to be?
- Did anything happen you didn't like?
- What will you do differently next time?

For example, did you join a new club at school to learn more about your favorite STEM topic? Or bake cookies for a neighbor? Were you nervous to meet new people or share something you'd made? After you went to your first meeting or dropped the cookies off, were you excited? Was it fun to do something new? Do you feel empowered to keep doing new things? Did the cookies bring joy to your neighbor?

SCIENCE • TECHNOLOGY • ENGINEERING • MATHEMATICS

Every chance we get to learn and grow only makes us better, even if the outcome isn't always what we hope it will be. When that happens, to keep from getting discouraged, it's good to remember that we're not sharing our gifts for our glory but for God's, and if something happened that we didn't intend, we can reflect on it, find the lesson, and do it differently next time.

# Part Two

*Fueling Your Superpowers*

Chapter 5

# Taking Care of
# Your Fizeek

*²⁹ And God said, "Behold, I have given you every plant yielding seed that is on the face of all the earth, and every tree with seed in its fruit. You shall have them for food.*

*Genesis 1:29*

Bella had always thought of food as just something to grab between activities or something her mom reminded her to eat during busy school days. **But one afternoon, after another**  energetic dance class, Ms. Nina introduced a new topic to her students: the connection between what you eat and how you feel.

"Your body is a gift," Ms. Nina said. "What you put into it fuels everything you do—from dancing to dreaming. Think of food as a way to honor that gift."

Curious, Bella went home and talked to her mom about it. Together they explored recipes and ideas for meals that were both nourishing and tasty. They decided to try making smoothie bowls that weekend. Bella loved the creative part—layering the bright fruits and nuts into colorful designs. As they ate, her mom shared a verse:

So, whether you eat or drink, or whatever you do, do it all for the glory of God. *(1 Corinthians 10:31)*

Bella thought about how food could be more than just fuel; it could also be an expression of gratitude for the amazing things her body could do.

The next week at school, **Bella started packing different types of lunches**—like colorful pasta salads, protein packed wraps, and veggie and hummus snack boxes. At first her friends teased her about her "fancy lunches," but soon they were asking to try her recipes. Bella saw this as an opportunity to share her excitement about food and wellness.

**Nutrition** is how our body grows and gets stronger. We need to understand what types of food it needs, what amount is appropriate, and at what times to get the most out of what we eat.

> **nutrition:** the process of providing or obtaining the food necessary for health and growth.

**If you have ever had and taken care of a new puppy, a kitten, a garden, or a plant,** you know that they need a certain kind of food in certain amounts at certain times to grow and get stronger. We are no different! Especially right now, while your body is still growing and changing, paying attention to your nutrition is vital. If we don't understand what types of food it needs, how much it needs, and at what times, then we could impact our body's ability to reach its ultimate potential both physically and mentally.

Food feeds and affects our entire Fizeek: our personality and emotions, our brain and how we think, our hormones, and our digestion. When we get the right types of foods at the right times in the right amounts, all our systems will be working at 100 percent. We'll have the physical energy we need to share our superpowers and the mental energy to think fast, whether in the classroom or out on the field. In other words, our Fizeek will thrive.

Planning ahead so you have time for breakfast in the morning, packing snacks for the day when you have a busy schedule, making sure you stay hydrated with water, or sometimes even bringing some sports drinks to replenish electrolytes and vitamins that get depleted when we workout really hard is essential for keeping your Fizeek going.

But how do you build a **healthy meal or snack** that will support your awesome, hardworking Fizeek? With carbohydrates, proteins, and fats!

# Carbohydrates:
# The Fuel for Your Fizeek's Fire

The first building block to a good meal and our main energy source for both our body and our brain is called a **carbohydrate**. You may have heard the nickname carbs. It is just a category of food, the first of the three macronutrients, and we want to be sure we are adding those into all our meals and snacks, especially the ones that are really close to when we start practice, rehearsals, or lessons. This is when we need the most energy to keep up with what we are asking our body and our brain to do.

What else did you notice about the word? Carbo-*hydrate*. Carbs actually hydrate our body, our muscles, our cells, and our skin as they break down. Not to get too science class about it, but as you can see below, when the first two molecular structures, called monomers, are combined, they release *water*! They are going through "dehydration" in order to become a more simple sugar that our body can use. Once those

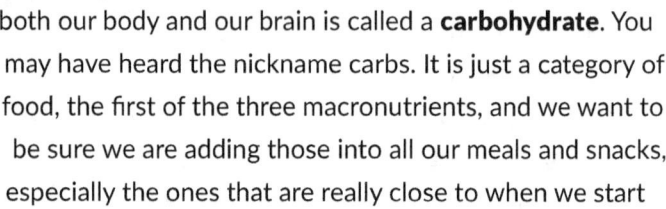

**DEHYDRATION SYNTHESIS**

$CH_2OH$  $CH_2OH$  $CH_2OH$  $CH_2OH$

OH  OH  OH  OH  $H_2O$

HO  OHH O  OH  HO  O  OH

OH  OH  OH  OH

glucose  glucose  maltose  water

carbs break down, they provide our muscles, organs, and cells the fuel they need to function and perform. Carbs fuel physical activities like running, dancing, lifting weights, playing sports. But they also give our brain fuel to make decisions, stay focused, organize ideas, and think through difficult situations. Think of carbs like little nuggets of energy that get released and provide power to all our essential daily activities.

> **carbohydrate:** carbohydrates, or carbs, are sugars, starches, and dietary fiber that occur in certain foods. The body breaks them down into glucose, which provides energy for bodily functions.

When we don't eat enough carbs, or when we burn a lot of them during exercise or physical activity, it makes us feel weak and sometimes even a little lightheaded because it also reduces our hydration. That's why it's important to get enough carbs in addition to drinking enough H2O (water) by itself. We also want to make sure we don't go too long without refilling those tanks.

Carbs come in two main categories: slow-burning (also called complex carbs) and fast-burning (or simple carbs—we'll get to these in a minute). Slow-burning or complex carbs take our body longer to digest and longer to break down, like in that chemical reaction above. The longer it takes us to digest and break down the carb, the longer amount of time we have that energy source available. Things like *whole* grains and *fiber* slow down our digestion, making certain carbs more slow-burning. Below are some great slower-burning, longer-lasting carb options to add into your daily meals and snacks or the grocery list.

## SLOW-BURNING CARB IDEAS

- Steel-cut oatmeal
- Whole grain cereals, like Wheaties (My favorite! But I also like Chex, Crispix, Multigrain Cheerios, and Puffins... Sometimes I even mix them together in my bowl before I pour on the milk.)
- Whole fruit, specifically apples, berries, oranges, cherries

- Sweet potatoes
- Whole grain pasta
- Quinoa
- Lentils
- Chickpeas
- Beans
- Brown rice
- Peas
- Whole wheat wraps or breads
- Frozen whole grain waffles

Sometimes, though, we need some quick energy. Think about after school right before practices when you don't have much time between last period and when you have to be ready for your after-school activities. We need something that gives us that fuel right away. These are called simple carbs, or quick-burning carbs, because they don't take long to digest before our body can use them for fuel. You might notice that some of these options fall under "junk food" or "processed foods" categories—that is where our Fizeek takes center stage. Sometimes we have to make certain choices in different situations, like when we need to perform. And that's okay. Think of these foods as more "energy foods," not "everyday foods."

## QUICK-BURNING CARB IDEAS

- Fruit snacks
- Applesauce or GoGo™ squeeze pouches
- Granola bars
- Rice Krispie Treats™
- Trail mix
- Goldfish or pretzels
- Dried fruits

- Whole fruit like bananas, grapes, mango, pineapple
- Sports drinks, juices
- Honey, maple syrup, or jelly toppings
- White breads, wraps, bagels

# A Note about Fruits and Vegetables

If you look back over the lists above, you will notice lots of fruits and veggies. That's right—fruits and vegetables fall under the category of carbs. Most fruits are quick-burning carbs because they break down quickly. They are easy to digest and give us that immediate energy we need to perform. Both fruits and veggies also do give us fiber though.

Unlike fruit juice, or things like applesauce, GoGo squeeze, or fruit snacks, when we eat whole fruits and veggies, it helps to support our digestion, keeps us full longer, and provides us with other *micro* nutrients like vitamins and minerals that we don't always get from more refined versions of fruits and veggies.

So when you are looking at your choices and making sure you are getting all those nutrition needs met, it is important that you don't rely only on fruits and veggies from juices, dried fruits, or supplements. We want to get those whole foods in there too!

While we're eating all these good foods, it is also easy to get stuck on the same fruits and veggies all the time. I love broccoli and apples, and I tend to eat those several times

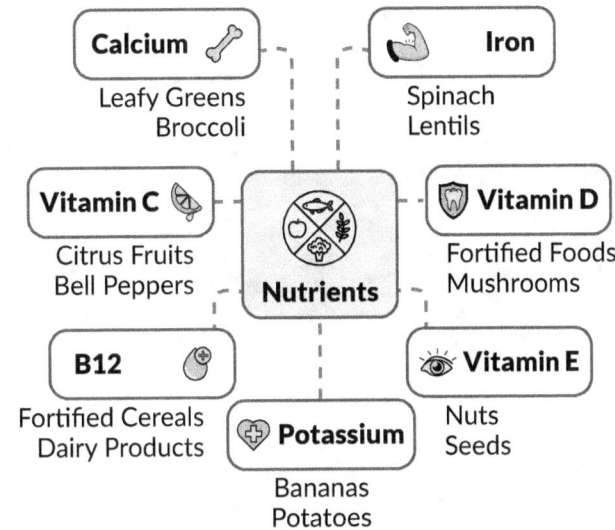

**Calcium**
Leafy Greens
Broccoli

**Iron**
Spinach
Lentils

**Vitamin C**
Citrus Fruits
Bell Peppers

**Nutrients**

**Vitamin D**
Fortified Foods
Mushrooms

**B12**
Fortified Cereals
Dairy Products

**Potassium**
Bananas
Potatoes

**Vitamin E**
Nuts
Seeds

throughout the week. But I have to remind myself that different types of fruits and a variety of veggies all give my body different nutrients. Some have more fiber, some have vitamin C, and others have iron or potassium. The more you can vary the sources, working in all the colors of the rainbow, the more you ensure that you are giving your body the full spectrum of nutrition it needs to thrive.

# Protein:
# Your Fizeek's Building Block

The second building block is **protein**—an essential macronutrient, like  carbs, and our body's rebuilding and recovery food. That means after exercise or in our daily lives, we want to prioritize protein (and your brain is a muscle that needs to be worked out too!). This is to give our muscles the nutrients they need to repair the breakdown and strain from physical activity (or from that really hard English test). Especially when our bones and muscles are still growing, we have to feed our Fizeek well to support every part.

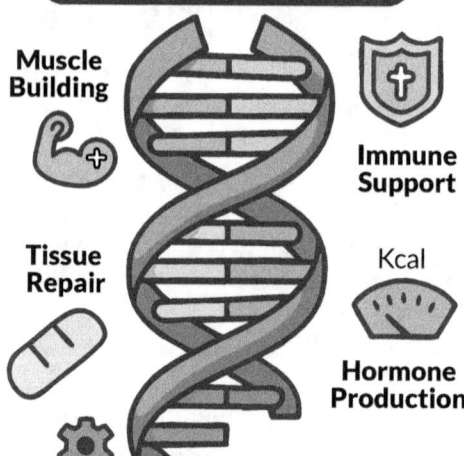

**PROTEIN'S ROLE IN TEEN HEALTH**

Muscle Building

Immune Support

Tissue Repair

Kcal

Hormone Production

Enzyme Function

When the protein in our food is digested, it gets broken down into building blocks called amino acids. There are twenty amino acids that combine to form different kinds of protein structures. Most of these twenty amino acids can be made in the body from other molecules. But there are nine *essential* amino acids that your body cannot make. So they have to come from the food you eat. That's why it is important to eat a variety of foods that have protein to make sure you get all nine of those essential amino acids into your body.

> **protein:** any of various naturally occurring extremely complex substances that consist of amino-acid residues joined by peptide bonds.

We usually hear about protein when we talk about body tissues, like ligaments, tendons, and muscles. But protein is also used in bone, skin, hair, and nails. Without protein, we would have no **enzymes**, hormones, or antibodies.

Clearly, protein is an important nutrient for the entire body. If we aren't getting the right amount from the right sources, our body might start talking to us. Things like nagging injuries that won't seem to heal, slow recovery from our practices or activities, muscle soreness that lasts a long time, or just feeling "blah" in workouts. These are ways our body may be telling us something is missing in our meal plans.

**enzyme:** in case you're wondering, an enzyme is a biological catalyst and is almost always a protein. It speeds up the rate of a specific chemical reaction in the cell. The enzyme is not destroyed during the reaction and is used over and over. Pretty cool, right?

Protein can be found in many different types and sources of foods, but there are some main categories that we can focus on to ensure we are getting enough of the right kinds of protein throughout the day and week in general.

## PROTEIN IDEAS

- Dairy: Cow's milk, cheese, yogurt, cottage cheese
- Whey or Casein protein powder
- Eggs
- Meat: beef, chicken, turkey, fish, pork
- Soy: tofu, soy milk / yogurt, edamame
- Legumes: chickpeas, lentils, peas, beans
- Quinoa

The best and easiest way to make sure you get enough protein is to have one of these sources in each of your main meals. If you can, it is extra important to focus on protein after your games, practices, or workout sessions because this is when recovery and repair is needed the most. We all want to have strong bones and muscles. We might even be spending time in practices or at school lifting weights, doing extra workouts, or working with a coach to build strength, agility, and speed. Well, guess what? If you do all that work in the gym, but you don't give your body what it needs to build that new muscle, your work will be wasted. One side of training is working the body; the other side is nourishing or feeding the body. You don't get stronger in the gym; you get stronger when you feed your muscles, hydrate, and rest. This is when your muscles can adapt, recover, and eventually get stronger.

# Fats

**Fats** are the last of our three macros, and it's one of the most important sources of fuel in our daily nutrition. Fats are a primary energy source just

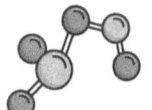 like carbs. In fact, depending on the intensity and the duration of your exercise, fats might actually be more important than carbs to keep you going.

> **fats:** nutrients in food that the body uses to build cell membranes, nerve tissue (including the brain), and hormones. The body also uses fat as fuel.

I know it is confusing because you also might think about this word when you think about having fat on your body, but these are two different definitions. Eating foods with fat does not mean they will make you gain more *fat*. There is a difference between *dietary fat* (meaning the fat you consume in foods and *body fat* (which is the fat we have on our body). One does not turn into or create the other.

The fat in the food we eat is a fuel source. In fact, it is the second in command to carbs. When we are active for a significant amount of time, our carb sources can run out, and when they do, our body looks for fat sources as the next type of fuel to keep us going. So just like carbs, we want to ensure we are providing our muscles and cells enough backup fuel in the event that we cannot always refill those carb tanks during long days or intense exercise.

Let me say one other thing about fat: fat is not a feeling. It is common in our culture to say, "Uggh, I feel fat." Especially among girls and women, when we have a big meal or eat a little more of something because we really love it or don't get to have it all the time (think **Thanksgiving** or maybe a **birthday party** when you have cake and ice cream to celebrate), we say, "I feel fat." But what we really mean is that we feel *full*, which is *normal* after eating.

We might be a little uncomfortable, even anxious or self-conscious. But the word *fat* is not an emotion. *Fat* is a noun, something we have on our body. Some of us have more, and some of us show it in different places. Your mom, aunts, teachers, or other older women in your life probably had more after they had babies. They might even keep it in different places now from where they did when they were your age. As you get older, go through puberty, and get your period, you'll notice things start changing on your body too.

Just remember next time you start to think or say, "I feel fat," there is probably a real emotion underneath all that. Challenge yourself to figure out what it is, and that will help you work through those feelings and resolve them.

Okay, back to the food facts.

Fats come in many different types of foods, just like carbs and protein. Fats are a little sneakier because often when you are eating carbs or protein, they also have some dietary fat in them. So you are getting a double dip! For example, **meat (like beef and pork), salmon, eggs with the yolk, nuts or nut butters**—these are all great sources of protein, but they also have fat in them. That is what makes them so filling and taste great.

Other foods might be carbohydrate sources first, but they can also add some fat to your plate. Things like bread or wraps, granola, chips, crackers, or sweets are primarily carbohydrate sources. But they also have some fat in them because of what was used in the baking or cooking process. Most of the time, the main sources of our fat intake come from the add-ons and cooking processes.

When we cook foods in **oil or butter**, this is also a great way to work some fat into our daily menu. Yummy toppings like **sour cream, guacamole, mayonnaise, Chick-fil-A™ sauce, or other dressings** will all add fats to your meal too.

Here is the **key** to making sure you work all these macronutrients into your day. When you build your plate (like we are going to do in the next section), think to yourself:

### WHAT IS MY CARB?

Rice, cereal, pasta, potatoes, breads, and fruits

### WHAT CAN I ADD FOR FATS?

Is there fat in my protein?

Or can I add dressing, oil, butter, condiments, nuts, or avocado?

### WHERE IS MY PROTEIN?

Meat, eggs, soy, dairy, protein powder

# Putting It All Together:

*Building Meals and Snacks to Support Your Amazing Fizeek*

What we want to remember about fuel is that it is important to think about and plan it when we have games or practices or are in the middle of our season. The night before a big tournament or the morning to tryouts

is when we want to make sure we are fueling our Fizeek with the best options possible for the activities we have to complete. The same is true for big tests or presentations, because our brain also needs the right types of nutrition and energy to stay focused and sharp, make quick decisions, and stay alert. Using this information, talk to Mom or Dad or whoever is

responsible for **grocery shopping** about what we might need to have in the fridge or pantry.

All this nutritious eating doesn't mean that "fun" foods and treats are off the menu. I'm a nutrition coach, and I cannot imagine my life without Twizzlers or Butterfinger Blizzards from Dairy Queen! That would be a sad, sad day. But I know that if I need to get a lot done or have a big meeting the next day, and I want to get good sleep and have the best possible energy, it might not be the best day for those kinds of treats.

The way to think about it is not "Can I have that?" or "Should I have that?" But instead, "When would be the better time to choose that?" Then you can make sure you are always prepared for the day and the activities ahead, but you also know that there is absolutely time and lots of opportunities to work in the fun foods too.

*Some Things to Try at Home*

So a sample day of eating *fit* for your Fizeek (i.e., you have a big game after school or a big test right after lunch) might look like this:

And a regular weekend day (eating *fun* for your Fizeek) might look like this:

## FIT FOOD MEAL PLAN

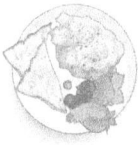

**Breakfast**
Toast with butter, scrambled eggs, and fruit

**Snack**
Apple with nut butter

**Lunch**
Turkey sandwich, carrots and hummus or ranch dip, chips

**Snack**
Protein smoothie

**Dinner**
Chicken and veggie pasta with red sauce and a little parmesan
*(everything is better with cheese!)*

## FUN FOOD MEAL PLAN

**Breakfast**
A smoothie bowl topped wtih honey and nut butter

**Lunch**
Chicken tacos or a burger with fries

**Snack**
A fun Starbucks™ or local coffee shop treat

**Dinner**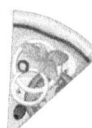
Homemade pizza with meat, veggies, and lots of *cheese!*

**Dessert**
An ice cream sandwich or other frozen treat

**Note:** *Since it is the weekend and you might sleep in and have a late breakfast, you may not need that midmorning snack.*

# A Note about School Lunches

School lunches are not always the best. (At my school, we generally had a rotating menu of frozen pizza, french fries, and some kind of hot lunch that I don't want to remember and probably never tried.) But once you have a solid foundation of knowledge about nutrition, you can be creative and design a balanced plate for your goals and your preferences. If you have a hard time finding choices at school, or aren't sure if you will like them, think about packing a lunch. Or at least take some extra snacks in case the cafeteria doesn't have a lot of choices that day or things are picked over by the time you get through the line. You don't want to skip lunch and let those tanks go empty. It is a lot easier to stay ahead of your hunger rather than trying to catch it.

# Diary of a Real Girl
## by Dr. Tiff

When I was in middle school, I was a very competitive soccer player. I played on my school team and on my travel team. We had practices for two hours everyday and played tournaments on weekends where I might have had two or three games on Saturday and Sunday. I was burning a LOT of fuel, and I didn't know then what I know now about the importance of what my body needed to perform and to recover. We would have fast food on the way to the fields. I didn't understand about hydration, sports drinks, or the importance of recovery.

I never put together that the way I ate, like pizza the night before a game, might contribute to getting hurt a lot. It also didn't occur to me that my lack of hydration and supplementation with electrolytes could have contributed to pulling my hamstring mid-season and soreness that lingered a lot longer week to week. I just thought this stuff was normal.

Instead, if I had refueled with some carbs at halftime to give my muscles a little boost of power, I could have prevented the muscle soreness from lasting so long. The same goes for celebrating between games. We all deserve to celebrate our wins, especially as competitive athletes, but timing them more appropriately could have done wonders. Instead of celebrating between games, I could have eaten in a more balanced way post-workout/game and saved the celebration for a day I didn't have to worry about recovery for more play.

This has led me to use the mantra, "What should I eat, when . . ." It gets me thinking about where Fit Foods and Fun Foods fit best depending on what I have to do that day and how it might impact my performance and recovery potential. (More on this next!)

# Diary of a Real Girl
## by Izzy C.

I have noticed that certain types of foods correctly fuel my body for my sport. Over the course of my food/health journey, through trial and error, I have realized what and when to eat certain foods. Where breakfast consists of protein, and carb filled foods, Lunch is a well-balanced meal with protein, a carb, and some greens, and lastly is dinner, which is about the same as lunch. An example of a good breakfast meal I have eaten is oatmeal with egg whites, milk or water, peanut butter, chia seeds, and any other toppings like blueberries, or bananas. A less filling meal that I and many others have had is a bowl of cereal. A bowl of cereal is not necessarily bad for you, but it is not the most fueling "meal" that will readily set you up for an action-packed day. Foods that are more natural and nutrient dense make me physically feel more prepared to skate.

I have also noticed that fun foods have a different effect on my performance than fit foods. To be more specific, a large amount of fun food makes a difference. I think that occasionally having fun food is healthy, and if anything improves your health and performance. A sporadic cookie, piece of cake, and a brownie is entirely okay. For me though, I have noticed that after a holiday/vacation of fun eats, that I feel awful once I am back to my sport. Last Thanksgiving I really let loose and had all the snacks, sweets, and pies I wanted, which is entirely okay. But I will say that my performance was negatively affected for about a week until I could get back into my regular schedule constantly working out, sleeping a healthy amount, and eating those fit foods that fuel me. It's always okay to let go sometimes, and it's also okay to be more regimented in your eating habits.

# Chapter Challenge 1:
## Fit Foods and Fun Foods

We've spent a lot of time talking about the science of nutrition and how it affects our bodies. So for this first activity, I want you to pull out your trusty notebook again and make a list of "Fit Foods" and "Fun Foods."

Like the sample menus above, "Fit Foods" just refer to things like complex carbs and good proteins and fats and "Fun Foods" are like my favorite Butterfinger Blizzard. You may even want to take it one step further and make your own sample menus with your favorite Fit and Fun Foods. One could be a "Game Day Plan," another may be your "A+ Test Plan," and another could be your "Sweet Saturday Celebration." That way you will have little cheat sheets and be able to look and find what you might like to have depending on your schedule and what you have to complete that day. And of course, if it is your birthday or a holiday, then Fun Foods rule! No questions asked.

# Chapter Challenge 2:
## Play Your Own Version of "Supermarket Sweep!"

Back in the 1960s, there was a game show called "Supermarket Sweep." Players would answer questions and play mini games to win minutes that they would use to run around the store like crazy, tossing everything they wanted into grocery carts. I know, I know. It sounds insane. But people loved it. For this Fizeek activity, I'm not saying run around the grocery store knocking stuff off the shelves into your cart as your mom chases you.

For your "Supermarket Sweep," I want to challenge you to help make the grocery list for your family, shop for the food, and then make a meal for everyone. Or instead of making a meal for your entire family (you may have six siblings, in which case, that would be a lot of food!), plan and prepare your own school lunches and snacks for one week.

# Chapter 6

# **Fueling Your Mind**

*30A peaceful heart leads to a healthy body; jealousy is like cancer in the bones.*

*Proverbs 14:30*

One afternoon, Bella and her friends noticed that they all started feeling tired and distracted by the time it came to after school activities and homework. When the Creative Writing Club planned a brainstorming session over snacks, Bella suggested they try making their own food for the event. Everyone loved her idea. **They spent an afternoon creating fun, high-performance treats like fruit skewers, homemade energy bars, and yogurt parfaits.** It was a huge hit, and Bella felt proud knowing she had brought people together in a new way.

Bella also learned to listen to her body. She started paying attention to how different foods made her feel and discovered that balanced meals helped her stay energized during dance classes and focused during writing sessions. She was even noticing that some of her emotions—like nervousness, anger, and sadness—were more under control. Every time she made a choice she knew would fuel her goals, she whispered a quiet prayer of thanks for the strength and peace it brought her.

By learning to nourish her body and feed her faith, Bella discovered another way to honor her journey—and to share that journey with the people she cared about.

It really is amazing how different foods can change how you feel. Some make you feel super energetic and focused. Other types of foods, or amounts of certain foods, can make you feel a little sluggish or distracted. Some foods keep us full longer, and others make us want other food pretty soon after. In the last chapter, we started identifying the connection between different foods and activities and how they can help you go the distance on important days (like the upcoming cross country meet where you'll have to run three miles!). In this chapter, we're going to talk about how foods affect our feelings and how to know if you are eating enough and the right balance of everything.

The most important thing is that you make choices that make you feel and perform at your best as often as you can! We want to be able to get to bed on time, fall asleep, and feel rested and energetic in the morning. We want to start our day with the amount and type of fuel that is going to give us good concentration and brain power in our first few classes until we get to lunch where we can "refill the tanks" to tackle the rest of the day, like after-school activities and studying.

**Listening to and honoring hunger** when your body is talking to you is super important. I like to think of it like a friend—you are building a communication process and a relationship with your body. When it tells you something, it is important to listen and respond consistently and appropriately. If you had a friend and they kept texting you about hanging out after school or on the weekend, and you never replied, what would probably happen? They would stop reaching out. Once that communication trust is broken, you have to work a lot harder to earn it back, right?

Our body is not that different. If you consistently ignore hunger or put it off time after time, and then feed it things that don't make it feel good or even upset its tummy or make it super tired, it's going to get kinda sassy. It might even fight back with getting sick or rejecting things. You know what I mean?

We want to build and keep the trust we have with our body and how we feed, hydrate, and take care of it. If we do that, then it will help us out too. It will be alert and responsive. All the systems will work together. Our emotions will stay level. Our skin, hair, nails, energy, digestion (aka pooping)—all things will be looking and feeling super energetic and healthy.

If we start to notice anything working differently or starting to **feel sluggish, foggy, or less sharp**, this can be a sign that we might just be burning a lot more than we are consuming. This often happens if you start a new activity or if your schedule starts to get super full, and then you don't have time to sit down for an after-school snack or if you miss lunch. Those things happen, especially as you get busier and have more social and extracurricular commitments. This is where we have to start to build some communication and awareness with our Fizeek. And it will talk to you, if you listen!

For example, if you notice that you are **sick or you catch colds** more often, this can be a sign of not getting an adequate amount of certain nutrients. Your immune system is telling you,

"Hey, we need a little more energy to fight off these bugs and bacteria floating around."

If you have been having really regular periods, and then all of a sudden, you start a few weeks later or you skip a month altogether, this can also be something to notice and note. A lot of my clients will keep a little calendar and put a star or a heart on the date they start just so they can remember their cycle and schedule. Sometimes when we first get our period, it will be irregular, and that is nothing to be concerned about. But once you have established a regular cycle, and then all of a sudden it gets a little wonky, maybe mention it to mom or another adult you trust to keep an eye on it. This could be a signal to look at your nutrition and eating habits.

Another sign that your body may need more fuel are memory blips and brain farts (yep, I said *fart*) like forgetting daily chores or missing an assignment or an appointment with your counselor or teacher. You could just be a little energy depleted.

Remember, one purpose of food is fuel for energy and performance. Food keeps us alert and on our toes when we are consistently feeding our Fizeek—the right things in the right amounts, at the right times.

If you do notice some of these little blips or symptoms, it's nothing to stress about. Just take a look at what is different lately or what has changed. **Have you missed any normal meals or snacks?** Have you been making different choices and need to add some variety back in? As soon as you make those little adjustments, you should notice some of those concerns resolving quickly. However, if you do notice the signs, and you ignore them or don't try and make those quick adjustments, then things can get worse over time. This is what we want to avoid.

Let's all commit to having a strong, open, and honest relationship so everyone can be performing, and living their best every day.

# Diary of a Real Girl
## by Charlotte B.

Growing up is all about being kind, responsible, and smart with choices. Healthy eating choices affect my life so much. My parents don't let me eat fast food, and I am completely okay with it. I mean, I'm not gonna die if I eat one french fry from McDonalds, or twenty, but you get the point.

Healthy eating affects our daily lives. To me, healthy eating consists of protein, like beef, chicken, even a protein shake a day; fruit, like apples, pears, oranges, strawberries, etc. "You have to have daily veggies!" says Mom. Cucumbers, carrots, bell peppers, and more! Veggie paradise.

If you live off of junk food, I've noticed you get in a bad mood. But, having healthy food keeps that good attitude going! Positive vibes practically are oozing out of you! Organic, healthy foods are what keep you going, what keep you awake and thriving! Junk foods and sugar will give you an hour or so, then you'll crash.

# Chapter Challenge:
## How Your Foods Affect Your Moods

Identifying how foods change your moods is a great way to start to learn about your own reaction, preferences, and performance foods. As you eat throughout your day, think about how your choices change how you feel. Here are some questions to think about to get you started:

• Do you feel energized, tired, or something else?
• Are there any times when you feel extra energetic or sleepy after eating?
• Do you notice that eating certain types of foods keep you more focused during classes or long homework sessions? (Think brain food!)
• When you don't eat on your normal schedule due to vacation, being out of school, or busy days of activities (missing a snack, or having to wait too long to have lunch), do you get irritable or "moody"?

Below is a chart to help you find the connections between what you eat and how it makes you feel. You can print this out and put it on the fridge or in your backpack. Pick some foods through the day, then identify how you felt about fifteen to thirty minutes after you eat them. The little emojis will help you identify your mood. You can also pick an emoji before you eat a specific food and one after eating that food if you want to see how it changes your emotions.

The bottom portion of the form is just a little space for you to list some foods you might like to try. Sometimes we get stuck eating some of the same foods all the time, and it is fun to challenge yourself to try new things. You can also keep some little notes of anything else that comes up either with the Food-Mood connection or as you try some new foods that might feel a little uncomfortable (or exciting) at first.

# FOOD & MOOD

*What I ate...*                    *How I felt...*

_____   ○ ○ ○ ○ ○

_____   ○ ○ ○ ○ ○

_____   ○ ○ ○ ○ ○

_____   ○ ○ ○ ○ ○

_____   ○ ○ ○ ○ ○

_____   ○ ○ ○ ○ ○

**OTHER FOODS TO TRY**              **NOTES**

. . . . . . . . . . . . . . . . . .     . . . . . . . . . . . . . . . . . .
. . . . . . . . . . . . . . . . . .     . . . . . . . . . . . . . . . . . .
. . . . . . . . . . . . . . . . . .     . . . . . . . . . . . . . . . . . .
. . . . . . . . . . . . . . . . . .     . . . . . . . . . . . . . . . . . .
. . . . . . . . . . . . . . . . . .     . . . . . . . . . . . . . . . . . .
. . . . . . . . . . . . . . . . . .     . . . . . . . . . . . . . . . . . .
. . . . . . . . . . . . . . . . . .     . . . . . . . . . . . . . . . . . .
. . . . . . . . . . . . . . . . . .     . . . . . . . . . . . . . . . . . .
. . . . . . . . . . . . . . . . . .     . . . . . . . . . . . . . . . . . .

# Chapter 7

# Moving Your Body

*²⁵ The way God designed our bodies is a model for understanding our lives together as a church: every part dependent on every other part, the parts we mention and the parts we don't, the parts we see and the parts we don't. ²⁶ If one part hurts, every other part is involved in the hurt, and in the healing. If one part flourishes, every other part enters into the exuberance.*

*1 Corinthians 12:25–26*

Bella dreaded gym class. She used to play basketball, but she just never loved the pressure of competition, and she really dreaded late-night practices. She wasn't athletic like Jordan, and she often felt like she just didn't jive with the team sports. But everything changed when her best friend, **Priya, invited her to a weekend dance class.**

"It's not about winning. In fact, there is no score and no judges," Priya said. "It's about having fun and moving your body."

Bella reluctantly agreed, and to her surprise, she loved it. The high-energy music and the freedom to just be herself through dance made her feel alive. It was like the physical equivalent to writing. The instructor, Ms. Nina, emphasized that dancing wasn't about being perfect.

"It's about showing up and celebrating what your body can do," she said.

That night Bella added to her prayers, "Thank you, God, for giving me this body that can move and dance."

Over time Bella noticed a change. She felt more energetic, slept better, and even started looking forward to gym class. She discovered that fueling her Fizeek wasn't about being the fastest or the strongest. It was about feeling good in her own skin—and taking care of the body that God had given her so she could keep doing the things she loved.

# Movement Matters

We talked a little about fitness in "Chapter 5: Taking Care of Your Fizeek," but let's dive in a little deeper. *Movement* is a pretty broad term, and it can mean different things to different people, but ultimately, moving your body through fitness or fun both have benefits. We move our body and push our physical fitness for a number of reasons, and those might change from day to day and even from week to week as you try new things and figure out what you enjoy.

Some of the top reasons to stay physically active are the following:

- **Improves heart health.** Exercise strengthens the heart muscle by increasing blood flow and heart rate.

- **Improves mental focus and capacity.** Exercise can help with thinking and memory skills, which can be useful in school and social situations.

- **Reduces the risk of depression.** Exercise can help you feel more energetic. Especially in the spring and summer, being active outside can help boost vitamin D levels and just give you a reason to be outside in nature, which also makes you feel good.

- **Keeps bones and muscles strong.** Exercise that involves some kind of impact like running, walking, or kickboxing can help with bone and joint strength, as well as muscle maintenance. Adding some resistance, like water (swimming), weights, bands, or even just body weight can also improve your strength.

- **Improves coordination and balance.** Exercises like yoga or pilates can help improve balance, coordination, and posture through core strength and flexibility.

- **Gives you a social outlet.** Exercise is a great way to meet people and engage with a new group of friends. If you join a team or an individual sport like tennis, golf, or cross-country, you will have a chance to practice with the other team members and make connections. If you aren't really into organized sports, but you decide to try a dance class or a yoga class, you will still be able to meet people and make connections in that community as well.

There are so many types of exercise it is hard to know what the best types are and how often and how long you should do them. The first and most important thing to decide is, what do you like to do? Because if you find something that you enjoy, which also allows you to be active for the reasons above, then you will be more likely to stick with it and stay consistent.

If you remember, I put food into a couple of categories, "Fun" and "Fitness." We can do the same for movement. There are times when you are moving your body with purpose. You are **working on a skill** for a sport or an activity, like a dance or gymnastics routine. There are other times when you just feel like moving your body for fun with no objective or goal. When I went to slumber parties in middle school and high school, we would divide up into groups of four or five and **make up dance routines** to songs. Then, after about an hour with our groups, we would perform the dances for each other. It was a blast. There were no prizes, and we weren't training for a performance, but we were moving our bodies and getting some exercise just by having fun.

There might be some afternoons when you don't have a lot of homework, you are not in volleyball season, or lacrosse just ended, so you have extra time. You decide to go to the park and just walk or ride your bike along the paths and sidewalks. If you like to **skateboard**, you might take your board to the skate park in the neighborhood to get out of the house and move after sitting all day in class. This is what I would call "Moving for Fun" versus "Moving for Fitness."

You can move for fun every day if you want. In fact, I would challenge you to find ways to move for fun throughout the day. When it comes to Moving for Fitness, this is where you need to look at how much and how often because it is easy to overdo it if we aren't careful, especially when we love our sport and are playing two sports at once. You might be running in cross-country because you really love running for your school, but you're also running in soccer practice a couple days a week because your travel team practices year round. This can be a lot to ask of your body.

Try and think about a couple of things if this comes up through the year. First, go back to the "Taking Care of Your Fizeek" chapter, and remember: the right foods in the right amounts at the right times will feed your goals and help you recover and perform at your best. If you have two **practices**, this means you are using up a lot of fuel, so you might need to sneak in a few extra snacks. Go back and check out the list of "Quick-Burning Fuel Ideas" for some good ideas to work in between practices or halfway through a long practice for that next-level energy boost.

Remember, if you want to elevate your game, you always want to be putting premium fuel in the tank. The quality of what goes in dictates the quality of what comes out in your performance on and off the field.

If you know that you are going to have some months with that packed practice or game schedule, you can also work with a fitness or strength-and-conditioning coach to help you better prepare for this type of demand. Our body is extremely adaptive. If we consistently expose it to more and higher demands, it will begin to get used to it. Pretty soon what feels hard, heavy, and long gets easier and easier. But you don't want to start working on this when the season begins. Especially if you are trying out something for the first time, the more you can get your body and your endurance ready ahead of time, the easier it will be to get into the flow of the season.

While there are a number of really positive benefits of movement and exercise, intense training is a form of stress. Every time we work out, whether lifting weights, **running**, stretching, or working on agility or speed, our body is getting broken down. This is why we feel sore and our body and mind are tired after long training sessions or by the end of the week.

**85**

A certain amount of physical stress is important because this is how our muscles and our heart learn to get stronger. But if we push too hard for too long without the right amount of rest and nutrition, the stress becomes too much. Learn to listen to your body—it is usually pretty in tune with what you need. And if we don't listen, it gets louder and louder until we do. This could be catching a cold or the flu, **getting hurt**, or just starting to lose our love for the sport. We don't want any of these to happen, so communication is key.

You might need to talk to your coaches about some rest days or a few days where maybe you have a modified practice, so you can still participate and be a part of the team, but you make sure you give your body a break. Just remember, a couple days of rest to avoid a week on the sideline is always worth it.

The most important message about moving your Fizeek is that you do! There are no rules; there is no better or worse way to do it. You find something that motivates you to move, and the rest will take care of itself. If you try to force yourself into a sport or an activity that you think you "should" do, and you don't feel excited about it, then it will end up stealing your joy. Find the joy in both "Moving for Fun" and "Moving for Fitness" types of movement, and do your best to find times for both of them every day, every week, and every season.

# Diary of a Real Girl
## by Karsen H.

I'm a competitive cheerleader, and I've been doing this sport for nine years now. Almost my whole life since I started at four! I've been super lucky to have some awesome opportunities to compete at the highest level in cheer, which has been amazing. One thing I've learned about cheer is that it's all about balance. You have to love being active and having fun, but you also need to think about the stuff you do outside of practice to keep improving. It honestly requires a lot of discipline and a love of being active and being pushed because it runs year round, and we spend long hours in the gym each week.

For example, the fun part might be stunt reps. We practice them over and over again to build strength and stamina for routines. Sometimes our coaches even make up games so we can practice different parts of the routine without it feeling like work. That's honestly one of my favorite things because it keeps everything exciting and fun. This year I am on two teams, and I get to base on one of them for the first time. These reps have been so helpful in helping me build the strength I need to be able to lift my flyer like I need to. As I fly on my other team, I also have a weekly flight class that helps us get good reps and clean up our technique, and we get to learn a stunt from another team. That is always fun!

# Diary of a Real Girl
## by Karsen H.     (continued)

But then, there's the less fun stuff like all the extra stretching I have to do as a flyer. I need to be super flexible to hit my positions in the air and make them look effortless, but stretching is definitely not my favorite thing probably because I am not naturally flexible. But I know it's important, so I do it anyway because I want to be the best flyer I can be.

Another less fun example is tumbling class. We often spend about ten minutes doing conditioning stations to get stronger. It's hard work, but it helps us improve our tumbling skills and get to the next level, but it is so hard, and I'm usually so sore the next day. So I kind of get fun and fitness in one class.

When I was younger, I didn't really think much about fitness or being healthy. But now it's super important to me. I've even started lifting weights with my parents or going on runs when we're not in competition season. I've realized that being active makes me feel so much better, both physically and mentally. I love to feel healthy and strong because it helps me feel better about myself, and I love when I can push myself to do something I couldn't do before physically.

So, if you ask me, being active for fun and fitness doesn't have to be two separate things. Finding something that combines both is the best. It makes it feel more like something you want to do and look forward to rather than something you have to do.

# Chapter Challenge:
## Movement Calendar

Sometimes we get so overwhelmed with school, extracurriculars, jobs, or social commitments that movement takes a back seat.

Then there are times when we are "all in" on our sport, and we never have time to move for fun. Or if we don't make fun or fitness a priority, all of a sudden, we realize a week has gone by, and we have not moved at all! Making a calendar and setting some movement goals is a great way to make sure we are moving consistently, we are moving in different ways, and we are moving the right amount.

Your challenge for this chapter is to make a Movement Calendar (template below) for the next thirty days. Each little bubble represents one day, and while there are thirty-one bubbles, that doesn't mean you'll use all thirty-one every month because not every month has thirty-one days.

# Chapter Challenge:
## Movement Calendar (continued)

Identify and write in the name of a "Moving for Fitness" activity in the right-hand column. In the example below, you can see I penciled in, "Soccer Practice." Start with the activities you've already committed to.

Then, identify a "Moving for Fun" activity, and write it on the left-hand column. I filled in "Daily Dance Party" for my "Moving for Fun" commitment in the example.

You can fill in more than one activity for each category or just start with one of each for the first month and see how you do. Each day you complete that specific activity, check a bubble.

The goal is to spend time moving in both ways every week. If you are an athlete in season, then certainly, more of your days and choices will be Moving for Fitness, so the challenge for you is to make sure you are reserving time to Moving for Fun. This will help with avoiding burnout and also give your body some different ways to recover and use different types of muscles. If you are not an athlete, this will still work wonders for you too.

# movement calendar

**FUN:** _Daily Dance Party_   **FITNESS:** _Soccer Practice_

○○○○○○○○○○
○○○○○○○○○○
○○○○○○○○○○
○

○○○○○○○○○○
○○○○○○○○○○
○○○○○○○○○○
○

**FUN:** _____   **FITNESS:** _____

○○○○○○○○○○
○○○○○○○○○○
○○○○○○○○○○
○

○○○○○○○○○○
○○○○○○○○○○
○○○○○○○○○○
○

**FUN:** _____   **FITNESS:** _____

○○○○○○○○○○
○○○○○○○○○○
○○○○○○○○○○
○

○○○○○○○○○○
○○○○○○○○○○
○○○○○○○○○○
○

**FUN:** _____   **FITNESS:** _____

○○○○○○○○○○
○○○○○○○○○○
○○○○○○○○○○
○

○○○○○○○○○○
○○○○○○○○○○
○○○○○○○○○○
○

# Part Three

*Sharing Your Superpowers*

# Chapter 8
# Perfectly Imperfect

*26 That means we will not compare ourselves with each other as if one of us were better and another worse. We have far more interesting things to do with our lives. Each of us is an original.*

*Galatians 5:26*

Bella was scrolling through her phone one evening, watching videos of her favorite influencers. Their perfectly styled outfits, flawless makeup, and confident smiles made her feel a twinge of envy. **She glanced at herself in the mirror and saw her messy braid**, the smudge of ink on her hand from writing, and her simple sweatshirt. A thought crept into her mind:

*Why can't I look like them?*

The next day at school, Bella noticed Priya applying a swipe of lip gloss in the bathroom.

"Do you ever feel like you don't measure up?" Bella asked.

Priya paused and smiled, handing Bella the tube of gloss.

"Sometimes," she admitted. "But I realized something. All those people online? They're just showing their highlight reel. You and I—we're the full story."

Bella thought about that as she walked to class. Bella started experimenting with her style—not to imitate the influencers but to find what made her feel good. She and her mom spent a Saturday browsing thrift stores, laughing as they tried on everything from vintage dresses to funky hats. Bella discovered she loved soft pastels and flowy skirts. When she looked in the mirror wearing her new outfit, she felt a spark of joy.

She also tried makeup for the first time, with Priya's help.

"Remember," Priya said, "makeup is just an accessory. It doesn't make you beautiful—you already are."

Bella practiced a simple routine: a touch of mascara and a hint of blush. It wasn't about covering up but about celebrating her features.

But even with these changes, Bella still struggled with comparison. One afternoon, during a Creative Writing Club meeting, she overheard a group of girls discussing how "perfect" another student looked. For a moment, Bella felt the familiar sting of inadequacy. Then she remembered what Priya had said: "You and I—we're the full story."

She decided to share her feelings with the club. "Sometimes I feel like I'm not enough," she admitted, her voice trembling. "But I'm starting to realize that being myself is more important than being perfect."

The room was silent for a moment, and then Elena spoke up.

"Me too," she said. "I think we all feel that way sometimes."

That conversation became a turning point. Bella realized that everyone had insecurities, even the people who seemed the most confident. She made a commitment to focus on her own journey rather than comparing herself to others.

To keep herself grounded, **Bella created a "Beautifully Me" board** in her room. She pinned up her favorite Bible verses, pictures of her friends, and notes about things she loved about herself. Every morning she spent a few moments looking at the board and thanking God for creating her just as she was.

# Embracing Your Unique Physique

Back in chapter 1, I introduced you to my word, *Fizeek*, and how it encompasses your amazing mind, body, and character. In this chapter, we're going to talk about embracing your unique **physique**—what your body looks like (not just its size but all of its parts), as part of celebrating your Fizeek.

> **physique:** the form, size, and development of a person's body.

For example, I am a shorty. And I have dark hair, but I used to have blond hair, so now I highlight it because I like it blond. My eyes are blue and/or green. If I wear blue, they look more blue, and if I wear green, well, you guessed it—they look more green. It's fun!

When I was in high school, and we had assemblies or chorus concerts, I always noticed **how different everyone in the line** was. Some taller, some with wider shoulders or hips. Some girls had really strong and defined legs. Some of my friends wore braces for a long time. Others never had braces. Our skin color also made us all different: white, black, brown, or a combination. And depending on someone's pigment, or the shade of their skin, they may get a little red or turn darker in the sun.

Your eyes might be beautiful brown or hazel. You may have super long legs or be short like me. You may have red hair (I've always loved red hair!) or deep-brown or black hair. Curly hair. Straight hair. Your skin may be lighter or darker. Whatever your personal physique, the best part about your parts is how unique and special they are.

# Beware the Comparison Trap

As much as we love ourselves, though, it's hard not to look around and compare ourselves to others, especially our physical body stuff because it's what we see when we first meet someone. Honestly, even if someone is your best friend and you get to see them all the time, you may wonder, "What would it be like to have that kind of hair?" or "To look like her?" But guess what? Your friend is thinking the same thing about you—could be about a different part of your Fizeek or even one of your superpowers: "Man, I wish I could sing like Sara," or "I wish I could run as fast as Hannah."

There's a famous quote that says, "Comparison is the thief of joy." Comparison takes away our joy. Did you know that? Think about it: you wake up and get dressed for school. You pick out your favorite outfit, with cool new sneakers to match. **You even had a haircut yesterday that you can't wait to show off to everyone at school.** You put on your shiny, new lip gloss (if that's your thing), and you hop in the car for school. As soon as you pull up, you see your girls waiting for you.

**Then you glance down and notice one of them just got new shoes too, and everyone is admiring them.** You look down at your feet, and suddenly, your shoes, your outfit, your haircut, and even your lip gloss don't seem so great anymore.

Then you think, *Ugh. Now no one will notice me.*

That simple comparison to someone else stole all the joy you were feeling on that ride to school. All the energy in your balloon just popped.

What if you thought about it like this: *Oh cool! Reagan got new shoes too! Now we can take some fun pics together and show them off. I've never really had a chance to talk to her before, so this could be a good way to get to know her.*

So the next time you feel yourself looking around and comparing, whether it's what you are wearing, how you fixed your hair, or even wishing you were taller like Morgan or could play guitar as well as Emma, take a pause.

Ask yourself what the comparison is doing to your energy levels, your confidence, your outlook on the day. Is it helping you or bringing you down? Is it building up your Fizeek? My guess is that it probably isn't.

The comparison trap is like quicksand. Once you fall in, you need to pause in order to think clearly and give yourself time to process what is happening. Whenever I fall into the comparison trap, I pause and remind myself that God made me just as I am. He picked everything about me for a specific reason, and He loves me no matter what shoes I'm wearing or what brand of lip gloss I'm using. And knowing that and feeling it in moments when I'm doubting myself makes a huge difference.

I have never been into clothes or shoes or purses or any of that kinda stuff. I don't wear a lot of makeup or read about new styles and fashion. **I work in a gym, so my daily uniform is joggers and tennis shoes.** My hair is up in a messy bun 90 percent of the time. I am not complaining; it is definitely comfortable!

**Yet when I go to meetings or events, I dress a little differently.** I don't change everything about myself, like my personality, my sense of humor, or anything like that. But fashion-wise, I have found my safe space, my happy medium. I let my hair down, put on a little lip gloss. I might wear a nice pair of black pants, but I still have on some sneakers and a half zip or some athleisure as my top. This allows me to feel really grounded in who I am while still dressing appropriately and in style for an event. I can walk boldly and live comfortably but still connect with the other people in the group. Maybe they have a different physical style or a different body type that looks better in certain types of clothes, but we find a common bond in the purpose of the event or the topics discussed.

Our physical body is just another way we separate ourselves and stand out in a crowd. If we start to understand our body and our preferences, find styles that compliment our shape and our uniqueness, then we can stand tall (or short!) and walk with our shoulders back and a big smile on our face. That alone will open the door to connect and relate to others in a positive, authentic way.

Here is the other option: if you are struggling to connect with others, think about what might be separating you from the people you'd like to get to know. Do they talk about topics you don't know a lot about? Do they shop at stores that you have never really tried? If there are things that you feel curious about exploring, and you think that it might open a door to build some common connections with others in a positive way, then maybe give them a try. The important thing is, though, that you stay true to yourself when deciding what changes you might make or things you might try. This is where knowing your core values will help *a lot*. But sometimes it is okay to try some new things or learn more about certain activities or **try on new styles of clothes that you feel good in.**

Here's an example: I took a drawing class in college to try and meet some people outside my normal friend group or in the other classes I was taking. It was a rough start. I think the professor tried to fire me a couple of times, but I kept showing up. I practiced every night, and because I was not an art major like the other students, I was able to connect by asking for their help. They felt needed, and I felt supported. While I will never have a career in the arts, I did end up with a final project that I was proud of.

# The Importance of Self-Love and Body Positivity

You might have talked about body image in health class or heard that term from a teacher or coach. This is a really important topic as we start to move into our high school and college years. Those are the years when most of us finish physically growing. We don't get much taller, and we know the shapes of our body and how all the parts are probably going to look for a while (i.e., all the things that make us the adult version of ourselves are pretty much in place).

But right now, you may look around and see that some of your friends have some of these characteristics and body parts while others don't . . . yet. I call them all the b-words (not *that* b-word!): *boobs, backsides, broader hips, body hair,* and even *body odor (BO)*. I know, I know. Kinda makes you giggle or makes your cheeks turn red when someone says it out loud. But as you get older, like Mom and Dad (or Dr. Tiff) old, these things are not that embarrassing. They just *are*. And the more you talk about them, the easier it gets. It just becomes normal.

The cool thing is that when these changes start happening for you, odds are someone else in your math class or on your soccer team is dealing with them too. Sometimes you are the first one. That is hard for sure. But then you get to be the one who helps everyone else deal with it when they are going through it. You will get to be the expert who knows all the deets. You don't need to announce it in science class or to your whole home room. My guess is, people will know.

So you just gotta own it. It is just how God made you, and the timing He has for your transition from a kiddo to an adult. You may be excited. You may be nervous. But everyone goes through it, and it doesn't last forever.

If you are the last one in your group to hit puberty, this is also pretty awesome. You get to learn all about everything before it happens. You can prepare and have all the info in advance. Plus, you get a few more months or even years before you have to deal with some of the not-so-fun parts of those changes.

If you are an athlete, this time can be a little challenging because everyone is getting taller or stronger or they might have a little more endurance—or maybe not. They might get stronger and have more muscle, but then they might not be quite as flexible, or they lose a little speed until their body and brain make that new connection. Anytime our body changes, we have to learn how to move it in this new way and adjust to find that coordination again. I have seen this happen in sports like cheer and dance or gymnastics. If you are a flyer or are doing the parallel bars, then you have a better chance to excel in certain aspects of those sports with your kiddo body. It just happens. But once you learn how to move the updated version of you, you may come back stronger and faster than ever.

No matter where you fall on that puberty timeline, there are going to be challenges, and there are going to be things that give you a leg up. Embrace where you are, and appreciate that all your friends, guys and girls alike, are dealing with the same questions and the same frustrations or curiosities that you are at that time. Be patient, be understanding, be supportive. And most importantly, if you see someone struggling, don't be afraid to ask, "Hey, how are you doing? I mean, how are you *really* doing?" (This is the question that will get the real answers.) **"Anything I can do to help?"**

# Celebrate Your Whole Self

There are lots of fun and creative ways that you can highlight your Fizeek and make sure you are taking care of it in a healthy way too. Depending on your parents or your cultural background, maybe even spiritual beliefs, there may be different rules and expectations about some of these topics. These are just some ideas and examples of how you could celebrate your Fizeek. But consider talking to the adults in your life, the ones you trust, and relying on your core values to make the right choices for you about some of the topics in this section.

## Hydration (Inside and Out)

We talked a little bit about this earlier in the chapter, but this is an important one. During this time, your skin is super sensitive. You are starting to produce more hormones and sweat more when you are active. You might have noticed some of those changes. When we start to sweat, and we have some of those new hormones in our body, our skin changes. It can change texture, meaning it can get really dry at times. You might have noticed that after a shower or when you spend a day at the pool or out in the sun, it looks a little scaly or has a white film on it. Dry skin can be irritating. If we leave it, then it can create some discoloration or other issues. Having lotion at home to moisturize your skin is a really good idea. Then, after you shower or spend time in the sun, you keep it hydrated. Using a lotion with SPF every day is also a good way to protect your skin, especially if you spend a lot of time outside.

Sometimes our skin can dry out or become dehydrated if we are not drinking enough water too. Make sure you are drinking lots of water and not too many drinks with caffeine or carbonation (like sodas and coffees) that can cause you to feel dehydrated.

# Makeup

If you are allowed to wear makeup, some brands and types will have a lotion or hydrating formula in it, and that can help with the skin on your face and neck (for example, products like BB creams or tinted moisturizers). But here's the kicker: sometimes we don't have dry skin; we have oily skin.

When we start producing hormones, for some people, this makes their skin more oily. So if you are someone who has more oily skin, and then you use makeup with an oily/creamy base, that can make your skin more oily. This is when things like acne and breakouts might happen. Especially if you wear makeup to school or sports practices or activities and you sweat. Now it's like a triple whammy.

One way you can try and avoid this, or at least make breakouts less frequent, is keeping some makeup wipes or cleaning pads in your school or gym bag! Did you know they even have oil-absorbing sheets? Keep a pack of those in your backpack for those super oily days. Then, if you do like to wear makeup to school or church or being out with friends, and you are going straight to a practice or game or just out to do something active with friends, you can take your makeup off before you start to sweat. You might still have some breakouts every now and then, but this can help. And as hard as it is, when you have some pimples or skin irritation, the first thing you might want to do is cover them up. But the more you can let them chill out and not put anything on top of them that can keep your skin dirty and irritated, the better.

I know zits can feel social life-ending for sure, but we have all get them. **I had one on my *eyelid*, seriously.** Just a few months before I started working on this book (yup, I *still* get zits!). How do you even get a zit on your eyelid? It was white and embarrassing, and I could not even put medicine on it because the medicine kept getting in my eye and making it burn. It was frustrating. But again, I just owned it. In fact, I even made a video for Instagram *with my eyelid zit visible*, and I just said, "Well, folks. Check out my zit. On my *eyelid*! I don't know how that even happens, but there it is, so if you see it or if you know how to get rid of it, let me know!"

Just by owning it, I released my discomfort, and I felt so much less anxious about it.

The reality is that people will probably see it and understand that you don't like it any more than anyone else. Just keep exploring ways to manage it and keep it under control.

## Fashion

Clothes are another area of self-care that seems to be constantly changing and constantly challenging! Some years the **jeans are skinny, then they are baggy, then they are bootcut** or something called boyfriend jeans—I don't even know what that means. Last year it was all about running tights, and all the pants were high-waisted. Next year it will be all about low-rise or something else. Long tunic tops were all the craze; now it's crop tops and midriff

hoodies. And that doesn't even cover skirts, dresses, and shoes. The options are endless.

Sometimes the styles that are popular, or that you are seeing in all the stores and all over social media, aren't the best style for your body type. Or even worse, you really love them, but maybe Mom and Dad aren't really thrilled about letting you buy them or wear them. Total bummer. Fashion can create some frustrations, especially when it comes to fitting in or feeling confident and comfortable in your skin.

Then there is the process of shopping itself. You hit the mall, you take tons of stuff into the dressing room, and only a couple of things fit. You might even try several sizes and styles, and it's just not your day. It can be exhausting, I know. I have been there. It happens to everyone, I promise.

Think about all those styles above that I just listed; there is no way that all those different types of jeans, lengths of shirts, or shapes of skirts and such are going to look great on everybody. Just think about your close friends alone; they are probably all shaped differently—different heights, different body types. So as the fashion fads come and go, different people are going to have way more options than others to pick from. Or you might just have to give in and decide if you would rather go with what's in style—even if it's not the best fit for you—or just stick to what feels and looks the best on your body—even if it is not the most "in" at the moment.

The most important thing to remember when it comes to clothes and shopping, and trying on, is that every brand and every store and every style is made different. **Don't worry about sizes and numbers.** They are just a way for the designer to organize their styles. If you have to go up a size or down a size when you shop, it means nothing. I would challenge you to not even look at sizes but simply get the fit that feels and looks the most flattering on your body. I bet if you look, most women have two to three different sizes in their closet, and they all fit! Some designers make clothes slimmer in the legs or broader in the hips; others might make the bust of shirts more forgiving, and others are a little more narrow. Clothes are meant to fit us; we are not meant to try and fit into clothes.

## Emotion Lotion

I know it sounds silly, but our emotions need attention and care too! If we neglect them for too long, they can dry up just like we talked about with our skin. It is really easy to focus so much on our physical well-being and care but forget to give time to our mental well-being and our emotional health. There are tons of ways to practice emotional self-care—or what I like to call Emotion Lotion, but I thought I would throw out a few for you to try.

As you know, I love to write, so one of the most effective ways for me to work on connecting with and exploring my emotions is through journaling. I used to start a new diary every year. I would write to it like an old friend. You might have tried this or even done it yourself, "Dear Diary..." and then you can just talk about all the things that are going on in your life at the moment. Did something funny happen at school today? Did you have a big exam? Was there an audition that you tried out for? What is happening at home? Are your siblings driving you nuts? Did you help mom with some chores and get on her good side?

The other way to journal is with a little more direction and structure. I know sometimes I sit down to write and just feel stuck. Nothing is flowing; the words feel confused in my head. So I keep a little journal by my bed or at my desk, with prompts. Prompts are like questions that just help you get the creative juices going. Often, I notice that once I get going, even with just a little nudge from a prompt, I can write forever.

There are lots of great devotional books available too, and while those are more specific to our faith and our mindset, they often explore a lot of our mental and emotional well-being as well. I bet if you jump on Amazon or even ask your Sunday school teachers, they might have some great ideas for a daily devotional to help with Emotion Lotion activities!

# Diary of a Real Girl
## by Macy W.

For the longest time I have spent my time looking at the influencers on social media and wanting to look perfect like them. They always have perfect makeup and are wearing the cutest outfits with the perfect hair. For a while I did try to be like them, until I realized that I'm, well, ME.

I love sending Snaps back and forth with my friends, especially my best friend Shyla. After we get home from school we talk about pretty much anything we think, while we wind down—taking off our makeup and changing into comfy clothes. Or, first thing in the morning when we're getting ready for school—think full-on heatless curlers, no makeup, still half asleep. If you looked at those videos you'd see me with no makeup, pimple patches on, in my favorite Bluey jammies (because Bluey is an icon) with my little sister running in and out of the bedroom screaming (and let's be honest, my mom yelling in the background for me to hurry up). I can promise you'll never see an influencer with all that going on.

Sure, I love looking good with my cutest outfit, hair done perfectly, makeup on just right, but honestly, my favorite version of me is the REAL me. There is nothing better than an oversized hoodie, leggings, and slippers. Especially after wearing my uniform all day!

So here's the thing: be pretty for YOU, not anyone else. No matter if you want some cute guy or girl to like you, they need to like you for who you really are, not just the part of you that you let them see. If they can't handle that, they can't handle you. God made you exactly who you are—embrace it!

# Chapter Challenge :
## The Mirror Exercise

This challenge will help you to see all the beauty that you reflect on those around you. All too often, the mirror is a source of self-criticism, a tool that we use to find our flaws or pick ourselves apart. "If only my tummy was flatter," "If only I had more defined arms," "If only my nose was a little smaller . . ." so many things we see and wish we could change. In this challenge, we are going to use the mirror to see all the things we are proud of, all the things that our body does for us and the characteristics of ourselves that we are so thankful that God has blessed us with.

One day a week, stand in front of the mirror. If you can, try and do it with as little on as possible. List five to ten things that you see and feel good about. It could be physical or nonphysical.

- I feel confident and focused.
- I have really good posture and stand with my shoulders back.
- I am really happy with how clear my skin is right now.

One thing I love to do is to use bright-colored Post-it notes and write those five to ten things down to stick on my mirror. Then, each day that week, I can remind myself of all the things I am proud of seeing when I look at myself in the mirror.

# Chapter 9
# **Believe in You**

*⁷For the Spirit God gave us does not make us timid, but gives us power, love and self-discipline.*

*2 Timothy 1:7*

God, give me strength.

Confidence didn't come overnight for Bella. It was something she built piece by piece, like a puzzle or a story unfolding over time. One day Mrs. Emory asked Bella to read one of her stories to the entire school during an assembly. Bella immediately had butterflies in her stomach, but she said yes.

**As she stood onstage, holding her story, Bella took a deep breath and whispered, "God, give me strength."**

She thought about everything she had learned: her superpowers, her core values, her physical strength, and the kindness she had shared with others. She realized she wasn't just telling a story; she was the story, a girl who had learned to believe in herself.

The applause at the end of her reading was like the roar of a Taylor Swift concert. For the first time, Bella felt truly confident in her own voice.

**Confidence** is a mindset, an attitude; it is how you carry yourself in the world and how you walk into a room—head up, shoulders back. It is a "swagger." I like to think of it as the action associated with the phrase, "Bring it on," like you are here for it, whatever *it* is. It's also believing in yourself or trusting yourself to meet whatever challenge is ahead. And it's something you can build and grow over time.

> **confidence:** a feeling of self-assurance arising from one's appreciation of one's own abilities or qualities.

Have you heard the phrase "Fake it till you make it?" Some people may have that calm and composed demeanor no matter the challenge. However, inside they might be dying. They may feel super nervous and unsure of whether they are ready or able to handle what they are walking into, but they don't show it, and they follow through with the commitment. Doing something even if it's scary or makes us feel nervous is one way to build your confidence. Because once you're done, and you see that you made it through, you feel accomplished and proud for persevering.

We all have a different level of confidence depending on the circumstances or the environment we are in. But beginning with less confidence than you may want is no reason to avoid something.

**For example, I am not good at video games.** I'm the one who takes down their own teammates (not on

114

purpose, of course) and who moves the controller up and down trying to make *Super Mario* jump instead of just using the buttons. It's sad really. And since I've had such negative experiences gaming, I'm very self-conscious about playing or trying to play, even for fun. Yet despite my low confidence in this area, if my nieces or nephews want to play with me, I still do it anyway. And maybe someday I'll win a *Mario Kart* race. Who knows?

However, when it comes to **coaching** or playing sports, bring it on! This is one of my super powers, so I won't back down to anyone. I walk into any game with lots of confidence because I know that I excel in this space. And that feels good. That doesn't mean I win every game every time, but I know that I have spent time building my skills and strengths, and I can play with the understanding that I'll leave my best self (best for that day) out on the field or court or whatever the situation might be. And no matter what happens, I'm good with it. (Also, a loss or a failure to meet whatever goal I might have set isn't a loss; instead, it's a chance to review my performance and come up with a different strategy for next time. Kind of like a scientific hypothesis. Make a plan. Execute it. Review the results. Refine the plan, and try again. This is another way to build your confidence because you end up getting better and better.)

When I am working with girls, or even moms, on the various areas of their own performance like sports or nutrition or mindset challenges, I often hear them say, "Well, I don't like to brag. That is why I don't speak up in class," or "I just don't want people to think I am showing off, so I don't really try that hard in PE."

Bragging or outwardly gloating to others about your accomplishments or putting others down to lift yourself up and highlight your achievements is one thing. But using your gifts, experiences, or talents to perform or excel in the classroom or on the field is not bragging or arrogance. This is what your gifts were meant for. Never apologize for giving 100 percent or for being skilled at something. Odds are in another class, or a different activity, someone else will shine brighter. That is how it works!

Arrogance, or bragging, is different from confidence!

Yet if you find yourself in situations where you are performing or putting forth effort *only* for the accolades or attention, you might want to talk to your mom or dad, coach, or teacher about your motivation.

***Do I really love this activity, or do I just need the attention?***

Sometimes it's both. It feels good to get attention for the things we are good at! And when you are good at them, you deserve to be recognized. We just always want to be sure we are not losing our true passion for something in place of external validation.

Also, getting asked to move up into honors classes, winning the lead in the school play, or being chosen for the varsity team or starting lineup are things we can all aspire to and be motivated to accomplish. However, if you are excelling in a class or doing really well in your sport and no one is giving you verbal "Yays," that should not impact your confidence either. Your confidence comes from within.

True confidence is knowing and believing in your skills and abilities no matter what other people say, notice, or acknowledge. A confident Fizeek speaks for itself! You own it, and God does His thing.

# Why Is Confidence So Important?

Developing a strong belief in your own value and abilities is a skill that you carry with you into every area of your life. The more you trust and believe that you can accomplish something important, the more positive energy you will direct toward that task or activity.

Let's say you decide to try out for the school play. You have never been to an acting class or read from a script or had to memorize lines. All new things! These are exciting, scary, and unfamiliar experiences but also a great new challenge. It is absolutely okay and normal to be nervous. You have done all you can do to prepare. You rehearsed at home, you set up a scene with your mom and sister to practice, you studied and made improvements each day. Most importantly, you have used your prayers to ask that God stand beside you on the stage, that He guide your words and your actions, and that He give you strength and confidence.

You then have to step back and say, "Have I done everything within my control to set myself up for success? Did I put forth 100 percent effort?"

If the answer is yes, then you cannot fail. If you give everything you have, that is already a success, regardless of the outcome! When you remind yourself of this, and when you realize that you are putting in the effort and making the most of the resources you have, that's an example of building strength and character you can repeat going into any situation that will continue to boost and grow your confidence throughout your life.

Here's the thing: if we stop trying because we don't get the outcome we want the first time, it might just mean that those specific superpowers could be hidden a little deeper than our other superpowers. They are waiting to be trained and unleashed. If we stop short, they might never have a chance to shine. What a total bummer that would be!

We have to keep working and growing and learning so those superpowers can thrive and be used to do more good and impact more people. **Until we unveil all of our superpowers, we can never embody our ultimate Fizeek.**

When we hit resistance or encounter a challenge or obstacle, it can be tempting to just stop and say, "This is good enough. I've found a couple of superpowers. I don't need any more. And because this [insert challenge here] is hard, it probably means I'm just not supposed to do this thing."

But the true sign of confidence is when we let those setbacks become our biggest comebacks! Our worth, skills, and value are determined by where we end up, not the path it takes to get there, not by how many detours or U-turns we make, but simply by staying the course and finishing the race. As we know from the Bible and from Jesus's ultimate sacrifice, the race is already won; the only way we lose is to stop believing.

## What You Think Is What You Get

We can all agree that God does not make mistakes. He created us on purpose, for a purpose. Think about every time you have negative thoughts about your looks, your creativity, how smart you are, or whether people like you. Even if those are private, inward thoughts, God can hear you. If we are created in His image, if He chose every special part of you for a reason, and you are questioning those choices, you are also doubting God. Those thoughts or criticisms are a rejection of His works in you.

Is it okay to wish things were different sometimes? Of course. Is it okay to question and wonder, "Why was I created like this?" or "Why was I given this challenge in my life?" Absolutely.

But question from curiosity and not judgement. Explore why you were created just as you are or why you were chosen for a specific challenge. There is definitely a reason. You may not know why today or even tomorrow, but someday you will. **So instead, try asking things like, "God, help me to see how you would like me to use this situation to bring me closer to you," or "How can I become stronger through this struggle?"**

One thing that is always really helpful for me when I feel myself getting down or beating myself up is to think about how many people have pushed through hardships so much bigger than mine. Some people struggle with learning differences; others might have physical disabilities that require them to have constant care or support. I have friends who have hearing or vision impairments. Their daily battles, even to do the little things that most of us take for granted, is a real challenge. When I think about these people, or even see complete strangers stepping up and showing up despite these daily challenges, I am so amazed and inspired by how strong they have become because of these battles. I am sure they asked God every day, "Why?" But if they were to really sit back and think about how strong they have become because of the mental or physical challenges they were given, they can see that God had a plan. We can all learn from those who have overcome and found purpose in their pain.

If you have ever gotten feedback from a coach or a teacher, you have probably had some feedback delivered in a way that really pushed you to want to improve or work harder. In other cases, you got feedback that was a real knock on your confidence and might have even left you more frustrated than if you had gotten no feedback at all. Our internal dialogue, or what we call "self talk," can have the same effect depending on if those thoughts are positive or negative.

The power of the mind is pretty amazing and hard to overcome. I like to say, "What you think is usually what you get." For example, if you say, "Don't think about purple elephants," what are you thinking about right now? My guess is purple elephants. It is hard to not think about something when the image is in your mind. This can happen with actions and outcomes as well. "Don't miss this foul shot!" "Don't forget your lines." "What if I forget the answers to the essay question?"

This is why we have to be very careful what we think and how long we dwell on it. The longer we give it attention, the more power that thought gets, and the more likely it is to become a reality.

One of the most effective ways of changing those negative thoughts into positive, motivating thoughts is a process called *reframing*. Reframing takes the negative thought that creeps into your mind and flips it on its head so it becomes motivation, direction, or information. We can then use this reframed message to change our perspective. Let's take the examples above:

- *Don't miss this foul shot!"* reframed: *Nothing but net. You have practiced all week for this moment.*

- *Don't forget your lines!* reframed: *I know my lines so well and can't wait to impress the audience with my timing.*

- *What if I forget the answer to the essay question?* reframed: *You studied and wrote practice essays. This test is going to be a breeze.*

We always want to be our own biggest fan. The internal coach that gives positive, directive, and helpful feedback. This helps us to grow and improve while also being motivated to keep moving forward even when it is hard. If that is hard to do, you can also think about how you would talk to your best friend or sister. How would you help them through a difficult situation or pump them up before a big game? This is how we should think about talking to ourselves. I would imagine there are times you say things to yourself and about yourself that you would never say to a friend.

Speaking of friends, peer pressure is another time when our confidence can really be tested. All of you and all the steps in your life are ordered exactly as they were meant to be. When we believe that God has laid a path down for us to follow, this is a significant step in our faith journey. But it is easy to stop there—*"Oh yeah, I know God has a plan for me"*—yet continue to go through life allowing circumstances or sometimes other people dictate your decisions. Sometimes we try to take control of the steering wheel. This is when we tend to get ourselves into trouble.

# Standing Strong in the Storm

Peer pressure is one of the biggest detours we can take from our walk with Christ. We can find ourselves chasing attention, achievements, or letting our emotions pull us off course. When others are veering off the path laid before us, it can be so tempting to follow them. No one likes to be left out from the crowd or, in some cases, miss out on what looks like a lot of fun. I for one love to have fun. Who doesn't?

It is hard to go against the crowd or rock the boat and be the one to ruin the fun. We often find ourselves standing in the middle wondering, *Which is the right choice? Do I go with the flow and build deeper connections with my friends? Or do I go with my gut and say "No thanks"?*

It is *hard!*

Believe it or not, I have been stuck in that situation, and I have made the wrong choice. I have since learned how to make the right one most of the time, but I am still not perfect at it either. So the best pieces of advice I can give are the following:

**1. Ask God for help.** Just be real and honest. *God, I am struggling here. I don't know which is the right choice. My friends are asking me to join them to go to this movie, and I know my parents would not be that happy with me if I go. But I am worried if I say no, they will talk about me, or they will all have something to talk about Monday at school, and I will be left out. Can you guide my heart and help me make the right choice?* Sometimes it is hard because the decision is something you have to make really quickly, but there is never too little time to stop and ask Him.

**2. Listen to your conscience.** If you are questioning the choice in the first place, then I would argue that there is something in your heart saying, "You know better," and the safest choice is just to say no. You might have other things to deal with later, but at least you have time to think about those and go back to number 1 with more time and less pressure at that moment.

**3. Take your own advice.** Put on your Big Girl pants, and imagine you have a daughter (or imagine your little sister if you have one) in the same situation. What advice would you give her? How would you feel if she went to the movie and you found out afterward? Often, putting yourself on the other side of the situation can make you see it from a fresh perspective.

We can only fully embrace our faith and our inner Fizeek when we stand up confidently and allow God to order our steps—all our steps. The way to confront and overcome peer pressure is just one of the ways that we continue to build and strengthen that part of ourselves.

# My Favorite Tools for Turning a Bad Day into a YAY!

Just because we do all the right things and practice and pray and pep ourselves up, sometimes the outcome does not go like we had hoped or envisioned, and it can end up affecting our confidence. When I'm having a bad day, it can be really hard to get myself back up, especially if I have bad thoughts in my head. It can feel like all the good thoughts get blocked by the bad ones, and the bad thoughts like to be really negative and persistent.

What do I do? Have a **pep talk** with myself.

> **pep talk:** a talk intended to make someone feel more courageous or enthusiastic.

A pep talk can be big or small, but I make sure I'm always ready with positive thoughts. For example, if my friend and I just got in a fight, and I'm really upset, I remind myself that it's okay to fight with friends and that I just need to give them a break. We'll still be friends; we may just need some time apart to cool down.

When I was still a student, if **I got a bad grade on a test**, it would be really hard to not get down on myself for it, especially because I was confident that I was a good student, and I knew I could've done better. But instead of thinking that I couldn't do this and just give up on myself, I would take a breath, close my eyes and say, "I know that was not the best grade, but I will get a better one next time."

Over time I've learned that the most important part of any pep talk is reminding myself that I can do this—I can do hard things, I believe in myself and my abilities to get better and better with planning and practice.

Here are some of my favorite things to tell myself when I'm down:

- *I am ready.*
- *I am capable.*
- *I am brave.*

Next time you're having a tough day, give one a try, or tell yourself whatever you think you need to hear the most.

Remember: failures are not fatal; they are feedback for how we can adjust, improve, and try again. Our response to the outcome is what strengthens our Fizeek.

My other favorite daily activity I call my "Yay of the Day." It is all about the little things, the things that make you say, "Yay!" I started this a couple of years ago when I had lots of heavy, not-fun challenges going on in my life. Some days it just felt like everything was bringing me down. So I thought if I could just find that little light in each day, it would help me realize that there is always something to be grateful for, something that can make you smile. I noticed the joy in things that used to go unnoticed or taken for granted.

- *Hey! My Amazon package arrived! Yay!*
- *Front-row parking spot at the grocery store! Yay!*
- *Seventy degrees and sunny outside! Yay! (I'm not a winter person.)*
- *My brownie recipe turned out perfect! Yay!*

I've done this for so long that it's automatic to look for the "Yay of the Day." I don't always say it out loud, but I definitely hear myself saying, *Yay of the Day,* in my head when something positive happens. I will even text a friend or my mom sometimes and tell them what my "Yay of the Day" was. Some of my friends and clients do it now as well. I smile every time I hear it.

So I'm going to encourage you to use it too. And if you want, you can email me and let me know what your "Yays of the Day" are. I would love to celebrate the little things with you.

## Strategies for Boosting Your Self-Esteem

At the beginning of the chapter, I mentioned the phrase "Fake it till you make it" and shared a couple of ways to build your self-confidence. Before we end this chapter, I want to share a few more ways you can practice self-confidence every day. It may seem silly that we have to work on how it feels to boost ourselves up, see our strengths, and acknowledge the things we do well, but starting that practice now will help you share your superpowers and strengths your entire life. Practice will make self-confidence not feel so uncomfortable and will help you get better at seeing your strengths and accepting compliments both from yourself and from others.

One of the most effective ways to start practicing self-confidence is with daily affirmations. These are the "I am, I will, I can . . ." type of statements that you can rehearse in the morning while getting ready for school or anytime you feel down on yourself or your performance (like in class, at school activities, sports, or in relationships). It really is as simple as just making a list of the things that you *are,* that you *can* do, and that you know you *will* accomplish when you put your heart and mind to it.

Here are some examples, give them a try!

I am a good listener.
I am a strong swimmer.
I am a helpful big sister.
I can read really fast.
I can make yummy cookies.
I can beat my brother at Minecraft.
I will make the basketball team this year.
I will get a part in the school play.
I will go to church every week.

Affirmations are one of my favorite self-confidence-boosting tools. Once I make my affirmations, I love to put them on index cards and decorate them, making them fun and creative. Then I carry them in my bag or my purse, and if I need a quick reminder of how awesome I am, I pull them out and read through them!

Sometimes our emotions can get in the way of our self-confidence or our willingness to really get out there and show the world what we can do. There are three things that cause us to get nervous, anxious, or experience more intense emotions:

**1. How familiar the situation is.** Anytime we walk into an unknown situation, environment, or a group of people we have not met, we get a little more uncomfortable. We are not sure what to expect; we don't know how they will respond to us or what we might talk about. So many unknowns. This happens every time you start a new school, move to a new city, or join a new group or team—even if you just go to a new place for summer vacation. Vacation is all about excitement, fun, and relaxation. But if it is a new, unfamiliar place, it takes us a little longer to get our bearings and feel at ease, right?

**2. How important the situation is.** Think about the difference between a pop quiz and a final exam: which one makes you more nervous? What about a scrimmage game versus the state tournament? You are probably going to be a little more anxious and excited before the tournament than when you are just playing against your teammates at practice. You feel less confident in your ability to rise to the occasion, to match the skill level of the opponent. And you are a little more nervous because there is more at stake. The importance of the outcome shakes our confidence a little.

**3. How prepared you are for the situation.** The last variable that affects our emotions and anxiety is how well we have prepared for the situation. Remember the example a few chapters ago about raising your hand in class after you had read the assignment and prepared so well for the reflection questions? You were not nervous at all when you threw that hand up because you had prepared! I am sure there have been other times (not many, of course) where you maybe skimmed the reading assignment. Glanced over the study questions. Were hoping not to make eye contact with your teacher that morning in class. Maybe strategically went to the bathroom just before the discussion began? When we are not prepared, our confidence plummets.

The best way to combat those emotions, and continue building confidence in these new and challenging situations, is to practice! There will be things you do and then think, "Uh, nope. Not my thing." But the only way you build confidence is to get more practice in uncomfortable situations.

The more we practice, the more comfortable and confident we feel in those competitive or high-performance settings. Start putting yourself in those situations that make you nervous. Think of it like a dress rehearsal or a role-playing situation so you can practice and prepare. And then, when it's time for the big game or important test or vacation in a new place, you'll be ready to handle anything that comes your way with confidence. The more we work through these scenarios, the better we can become at overcoming the fears and facing the fire.

# Diary of a Real Girl
## by Mackenzie

A couple of challenges I have faced are not putting pressure on myself to be perfect and to not upset anyone. I don't like messing up, but I have learned that it is ok to make mistakes because I learn from them and grow stronger.

I'm a people pleaser, so I don't like making people upset, and it's a struggle for me to use my voice and say what I want. But I think this year I have become more confident, and I have gotten better at not always doing what others want rather than what I want. I give myself the pep talk that

God is with me in
everything I do, and He makes
everything happen for a reason. So
even if things don't turn out how I want
them to, or if I'm nervous about something, I
remind myself that God is with me, and He has
a plan.

# Chapter Challenge 1:
## Your Personal Affirmations

Just like the "Real Girl" entry above, let's come up with our own pep talk! Something that you can remember and easily say to yourself when you feel some of those feelings of self-doubt start bubbling up. Or when the negative self talk starts creeping in. Remember, we cannot "stop thinking," but we can decide how we respond to those thoughts.

If we are in a situation that is difficult, new, or just really high-pressure, this is when that pep talk will come in handy. One of the best ways to start writing your pep talk is to go back to the section about affirmations, the "I am," "I can," and "I will" statements. Make a list of those below.

I can _____     I can _____

I can _____     I can _____

I am _____      I am _____

I am _____      I am _____

I will _____    I will _____

I will _____    I will _____

# Chapter Challenge 2:
## Write Your Personal Power Statement

Now we are going to write our personal power statement. This is similar to an affirmation; only it is one phrase that truly encompasses the person or the attitude that you want to show up with every day. A statement that always brings you back to center. This Power Statement is our go-to mantra to bring positive, optimistic, self-empowering energy to our day. We're not writing books here, but if you feel so inspired, go for it. Instead, we're going to develop a short phrase or mantra that reflects our core values and personality. For example, "Be the person God created you to be for yourself and for those who need it."

Once you've come up with your phrase, write it somewhere you will see it every day and be inspired to live up to it. That could be on your bathroom mirror (I love those markers that write on glass!) You could put it on a ribbon for your backpack or on a piece of tape that you stick on the handle of your tennis racket or golf club. Get creative, but make it powerful!

# Chapter 10

# Connect with Kindness

*³²Be kind to one another, tenderhearted, forgiving one another, as God in Christ forgave you.*

*Ephesians 4:32*

Remember Mrs. Emory, Bella's teacher? Well, she often said, "Kindness is the glue that holds us together."

Whenever Mrs. Emory said this, Bella rolled her eyes. *So cliché, Mrs. Emory!* But then Bella decided to put this lesson into practice. (And stopped rolling her eyes at Mrs. Emory).

One day Bella noticed a new girl, Amina, sitting alone during lunch. Remembering how she used to feel out of place, **Bella invited Amina to join her table.** They bonded over a shared love of books and became fast friends.

When the Creative Writing Club needed more members for their next project, Bella encouraged Amina to join. Though Amina was hesitant at first, Bella's encouragement helped her step out of her shell. Watching Amina grow more confident made Bella realize how rewarding it was to lift others up. It was so incredible to her how when you do something to make someone smile, it makes you smile too!

While it may sound simple, kindness is one of the most powerful gifts we can all cultivate and share. It taps into our ability to **empathize** with others (to feel how they're feeling) and help them not feel so alone or so invisible in the world. (And it usually makes you feel special too because you've helped someone feel loved as you are loved!) Even though it's simple, we don't always remember to share it or show it. There are a hundred reasons we should always choose kindness, especially when it's hard, but for now, I'll just share six.

> **empathy:** the ability to understand and share the feelings of another.

## Kindness:

**1. Builds connections.** When you're kind, you naturally attract others. People want to be around those who make them feel good, which can lead to meaningful friendships and a positive reputation. By being kind, you build trust and respect with those around you, making it easier to work well together, whether in school, sports, or other activities.

**2. Inspires change.** Believe it or not, kindness is contagious, meaning it catches on! When you show kindness, others see it and often feel inspired to be kind as well. Imagine if everyone in your school practiced kindness. It could change the whole climate, making it a friendlier, more supportive place. By setting that example, you're helping to create a positive change.

**3. Shows strength.** Sometimes kindness requires courage. It can be hard to be the one who speaks up for someone else, offers help, or treats everyone with respect—even those who might not treat you well. When people see you standing up with kindness, they admire that strength and feel inspired to follow your lead.

**4. Makes others feel valued.** People remember how you make them feel. By being kind, you make others feel valued and seen. Whether it's a smile, a helpful gesture, or a friendly "hello," these actions show people that you truly care. Even after you leave, the kindness you showed can linger for way longer!

**5. Helps you feel better too.** Science even shows that being kind makes you feel happier and less stressed. When you do something nice for someone else, your brain releases "feel-good" chemicals. So you're not only helping others—you're also helping yourself feel better.

**6. Sets you apart.** Not everyone chooses kindness, so when you do, you're showing something exceptional about yourself. While some people might focus on being popular, looking a certain way, or standing out in other ways, kindness is a trait that never goes out of style and truly makes you shine.

Next time you're in a situation where you can choose kindness, go for it! It's one of the easiest ways to make a difference in someone's day and to stand out in a meaningful way. Plus, the more you practice kindness, the more it becomes a natural part of who you are. Keep being awesome, and spread that kindness!

# Kindness in Action
## The Power of a Book

When Dylan Siegel was in first grade, he learned that his friend Jonah Pournazarian had a rare and potentially lethal liver disease with no known cure. Dylan decided to raise money to find a cure.

His mother suggested a bake sale, but instead, **Dylan wrote a book dedicated to Jonah** and got his school to make copies. By the end of the first week, he had sold enough copies to make $5,000, an astonishing business venture for a first-grader. It was a good start, but Dylan had his sights set on raising $1 million.

Two years later, with the help of his parents and others, he surpassed that million-dollar goal. With that money, doctors are now planning human trials for a gene therapy and saying, "We are on the verge of curing or treating this disease, and that would not have been possible if a six-year-old boy hadn't created this book."[1]

## The Power of a Dinner Table

Parents Kathy Fletcher and David Simpson adopted what's become known as Thursday Night Dinner after their son invited a friend, who sometimes went to school hungry, home for dinner. Word spread from that friend to another, and soon kids were showing up for what's described as "a **diverse, weekly gathering** that builds trust, breaks down barriers and establishes relationships rooted in love and high expectations and aimed at building the support networks our kids need to succeed."

The community blossomed beyond the dinner table into a nonprofit organization called AOK[2], which stands for All Our Kids, that provides more comprehensive support to current AOK kids and many more who need it.

## Pay It Forward

Laura Robinson was rushing from her daughter's ballet lesson to her son's football training when she made a quick stop at a gas station along the way. She hadn't realized, though, that she'd left her purse and bank card at home. While apologizing to the cashier and trying to arrange a way she could go home to get the money to fix the situation, a gentleman who had only popped in for a coffee ended up **paying her entire bill**. She asked him if she could send him a bank transfer for the exact amount. He said no and added, "One day you can do the same for somebody else."[3]

Each of these stories start from one small act of kindness that grew bigger out in the world. Dylan's book for his friend Jonah began as a small project in his school and grew into an opportunity to cure or treat a deadly disease. Dinner at a friend's house turned into a nationwide movement to help others. Covering a small cost changed the trajectory of someone's day. When you're acting from kindness, it's impossible to understand how big of an impact you're making on the world. But your love ripples out from that one small thing, creating big waves in the lives of others. Never underestimate the power of one small act.

# The Kindness Connection

Even when kindness connects us with people, those connections may still come and go. Girlfriends, guy friends, more than friends, friends. It is complicated and exciting. Here is the thing about making connections:

**1. It's normal for connections to come and go.** It doesn't mean there's something wrong with you or that either person in the relationship necessarily did anything wrong. It simply means you're growing up or that your interests, values, or even just your schedules might have shifted.

**2. Just let things settle.** In time your friendships will become more solid, and God will make it clear who is good for you and meant to be in your life. Be patient, pray for good friends, and pray that you will be a good friend. Remember that true friends are worth the wait.

**3. Just be you, and the right people will come along.** There's a saying that "Birds of a Feather Flock Together." That just means that people will inevitably seek out others who are similar to them. So when you treat people well, you'll attract friends who treat you well too.

If you continue to live up to the standards that God has set for us, and you show the world those superpowers without hesitation or compromise, people will be drawn to you. Your purpose has power— use it!

# How Values Influence Decisions and Friendships

Have you ever clicked with someone right away and thought, *Wow, it's like we've been friends forever?*

That's probably because you share similar core values. And guess what? Kindness is a core value! Usually, the people we form beneficial, strong relationships with come down to our beliefs and often our core

values. The people who share the same values tend to be the people who will understand you and that you will connect with on a deeper level.

Here's how core values play a big role in friendships:

- **They help you connect.** When you meet someone who cares about the same things you do, it's easy to bond. For example, if both of you love volunteering at local charities or going on mission trips, you might be able to do this together or support each other's passions and superpowers.

- **Values guide choices.** Imagine you're hanging out with friends, and someone suggests doing something that doesn't feel right, like gossiping about another person. If honesty and kindness are core values for you, you'll know that's not the kind of behavior you want to be part of. You might just decide to say, "No, thanks," next time you get invited to hang out or sit with them at lunch.

- **They keep your friendships strong.** Real friends respect your values. If being honest is super important to you, a good friend will always tell you the truth—even if it's hard. And being honest also means that you stay true to yourself even when it's uncomfortable, because you know they will still be your friend and appreciate that you are being real.

When you read these three bullet points, do you see the foundation of core values that we talked about in chapter 3? Pretty cool how things keep showing up. It's like they all fit together to help us put the pieces in place and ensure that we are building a relationship with who we are, who God has designed us to be, but also relationships with the people who come into our lives and share those same goals! Win-win-win. I love winning.

Now, it is important that you recognize and remember that sometimes we meet people who don't share those values *yet*, but we can be the way for them to find their relationship with God, maybe for the first time. It is okay to befriend, and connect with, others who have different beliefs. We just always want to remain strong in our beliefs and values, even as we respect the freedom to have different perspectives on the same topics. Kindness is the key.

# Diary of a Real Girl
## Lauren W.

I was bullied from second grade, all the way to seventh grade, but it really started to pick up in middle school. It didn't always look like what people would think bullying is. Many times it would just be excluding me from a conversation or play. A girl would twist my words, and she would turn people against me, resulting in me having no friends at school.

But, having no one to talk to, I had a lot of time to think—to think about my life, how I can be a better friend, etc. But what I found myself thinking about most was my spiritual relationship with God, which helped the bullying not affect me as much. It helped me focus on the positive, and ultimately, helped my relationship grow.

I moved states in eighth grade, so I moved to a new school where people are much kinder, and I have friends now. Sure, there are some people who occasionally give me looks that aren't kind, or whisper things under their breath, but I have learned how to look past them and focus on other things. I've become stronger because of what I went through. I like to think about my experience like the story of Job. He was faithful to God, and Satan tested his faith. Job stayed faithful to God through the challenges and eventually, the test ended. My test has ended, and I am more prepared for the next one because of my experiences.

# Diary of a Real Girl
## by Keller B.

Kindness is a really special way for me to connect with others and make friends. I've seen how simple things, like sharing a smile or saying something nice, can brighten someone's day. I remember helping a classmate with her homework once, and seeing how happy she was when she finally understood it. It reminded me how much it means to show that we care about each other. When I show kindness, it makes me feel good, too! Helping someone brings me joy, and I feel proud of myself. I've noticed that when I'm kind, it encourages my friends to do the same, creating a friendly community where we all support each other. Someone being kind to you is just as great. I love it when someone shares their snack with me or gives me a compliment. It makes me feel loved and reminds me that I'm not alone. These little acts of kindness help me feel more confident and make my friendships stronger. In places like school or on sports teams, kindness really matters. I recently switched softball leagues and when a new teammate asked me my name, or said something kind, it made me feel like I belonged! Sometimes, being kind does a lot more than you might think too. Maybe someone is having a bad day and feels lonely, your kindness could make their day 10 times better. When everyone treats each other with kindness, it creates a happy community. People seem happier and more willing to work together, and that leads to better teamwork and more fun! In short, kindness is super important for making friends and feeling connected. Whether I'm giving or receiving kindness, it helps me feel respected and valued. By being kind to each other, we really can make the world a happier place!

# Chapter Challenge:
## Acts of Kindness That Lift Others Up

*"I've learned that people will forget what you said, people will forget what you did, but people will never forget how you made them feel."*
— Maya Angelou

In this chapter, we've learned about the importance of kindness and how it can make the world a better place. So now I want to challenge you to commit a <u>Daily Act of Kindness</u>. Below is a list of actions you could choose from for your daily act, but these are certainly not the only things you could do. Every morning, choose one thing and write it down in the journal you've been keeping. Then, at the end of the day, reflect on it.

Were you nervous before doing it? How did it affect the other person? How did it make you feel? Would you do it again?

1. Do something nice to welcome your neighbors.
2. Keep an eye out for people who need help.
3. Give up your seat on the bus or in the classroom.
4. Visit your friends unexpectedly.
5. Acknowledge everyone you interact with.
6. Let other people be kind to you.
7. Connect with someone who hasn't heard from you in a while.
8. Flash a smile.
9. Take a moment to write back.
10. Say good morning, even to strangers.
11. Bring someone new to the lunch table.
12. Bake cookies for the cafeteria workers and/or janitorial staff at your school.
13. Invite a new kid to your house for dinner (with your parents' permission, of course).
14. Leave a note of encouragement or kindness for someone who may be struggling.
15. Join the tutoring team at your school to help someone in a subject where you excel.

# Chapter 11

# **Powered by Personality**

*¹⁷ As iron sharpens iron, so one person sharpens another.*

*Proverbs 27:17*

One day, during lunch, Bella overheard some classmates talking about an upcoming personality quiz in their social studies class. The quiz was designed to help students identify their strengths and leadership styles. Bella was curious. She had always thought of herself as quiet and a little shy. Would the quiz confirm that?

To her surprise, **the quiz revealed that Bella was a "visionary thinker,"** someone who could see the big picture and inspire others. At first, she wasn't sure if that description fit her. But then, she

thought about how her stories had inspired her Creative Writing Club and how her play had built a sense of community in the school.

Bella prayed her bedtime prayers that night as always, this time asking for wisdom to embrace her strengths. For the first time, she began to see her quiet nature not as a weakness but as a strength. She didn't have to be the loudest voice in the room to make an impact. Her personality was another superpower.

Our personality is the collection of characteristics and behaviors that make up how we show up in life. This includes major traits, interests, drives, values, self-concepts, abilities, and emotional patterns. Social scientists have studied personality for decades and have found that the differences between people's personalities can be broken down in terms of five major traits—often called the "Big Five."[4] Each one reflects a key part of how a person thinks, feels, and behaves. The Big Five traits are the following:

- Openness to experience (includes aspects such as intellectual curiosity and creative imagination)
- Conscientiousness (organization, productiveness, responsibility)
- Extroversion (sociability, assertiveness; its opposite is introversion)
- Agreeableness (compassion, respectfulness, trust in others)
- Neuroticism (tendencies toward anxiety and depression)

Self-evaluation (meaning, sitting with yourself and your thoughts) and taking an honest look at which of the Big Five sound most like you can be an invaluable tool. It is important to understand our tendencies—how we respond most naturally in certain situations. Once we self-evaluate, we have a more complete picture of the types of activities that might fit us best.

Openness to experience, for example, might be something beneficial on a summer mission trip. Extroversion might be a great skill for being in a

Girl Scout group or heading up a social committee at school.

Our Big Five traits can also inform us about the way we learn most easily and how we like to communicate, or be communicated to. Agreeableness would be a really helpful trait if you are working with groups, especially in groups where everyone comes from a different background or different skill levels.

You might have higher neuroticism if you tend to get nervous easily—for example, when you meet new people or there are unexpected changes in your schedule (your appointment gets changed or assignments get moved around on the syllabus). Knowing that you scored higher on this Big Five trait can allow you to put additional resources in place before big tests, or when you know that there is a transition on the horizon.

When you look at this list, don't think of it as "good" or "bad," like you should have certain traits or other traits are better or worse. The key is to increase your awareness and understanding of these five areas, so that you can more easily deal with situations that might not be naturally comfortable for you.

# Understanding Personality Traits: Introversion vs. Extroversion

One of the most common traits of the Big Five is extroversion, which then leads to its opposite, introversion. Take a peek back at the definition of *extroversion*.

> **extroversion:** the state of or tendency toward being predominantly concerned with and obtaining gratification from what is outside the self: a personality trait or style characterized by a preference for or orientation to engaging socially with others

Do you think you are **introverted** or extroverted? Have you ever heard those words before? Or are you thinking, *Dr. Tiff, what are you even talking about? Like, can I introvert my legs back behind my head or flex my body in a certain way?* It definitely sounds like some kind of high-level dance move. *The introverted double toe loop—not a thing.*

> **introversion:** the state of or tendency toward being predominantly concerned with and obtaining gratification from one's own mental life : a personality trait or style characterized by a preference for or orientation to one's own thoughts and feelings

No, those terms describe how you feel around other people, how you participate in class, or if you like doing things that bring attention to yourself (like performing onstage by singing or acting). If you read the definitions and you still aren't sure, this list might help! Read through them, and see if one sounds more like you.

## CHARACTERISTICS OF AN INTROVERT

- Cautious, likes to assess a situation before taking action
- Thinks before they speak
- Can concentrate on one thing for an extended period
- Listens and gathers and processes information before forming an opinion
- Has a calm attitude, prefers less-stimulating environments
- Likes to play and learn independently; self-starter
- May prefer writing and drawing to speaking
- Able to put themselves in the place of others, possesses empathy

An introverted person is usually a little shyer. They are the types of people who are more apt to have small groups for birthday celebrations or like to take classes with less students. They might be more interested in individual sports like tennis or golf. Or they might not really be into sports at all because they are timid and independent. Introverts are typically more drawn to self-guided activities like video games or art. They thrive in quiet settings where they can have more time to think about what they want to say and maybe don't have to fight or talk over others.

## CHARACTERISTICS OF AN EXTROVERT

- Risk-taker, likes to try new things
- Enthusiastic, engaging
- Easily adapts to new people and new situations
- Verbal communicator
- Thinks and acts quickly
- Likes to interact with others, affectionate
- Spontaneous, changes their mind often
- Can work with others to find solutions to problems and conflict

Extroverts are more talkative in groups. When there is a question posed to lots of people, they might be one of the first to speak out or throw their hand up. Extroverts like group activities and team sports like basketball, soccer, or lacrosse. They might even want to get involved in theater so they can be in front of people onstage or have a solo in the school musical. In class, they never mind being called out to present first.

The characteristics above are just "typically" the case. There are lots of introverts who are amazing singers and actors/actresses. There are extroverts on the PGA tour or who are master chess champions. There are introverts who have tons of friends and love to go to big group gatherings. And there are extroverts who live a very independent life and are not always interested in being around tons of people. You find your sweet spot or sometimes learn to step out on faith and do the things that don't come naturally, remembering who is always standing by your side.

Here are some of the most famous people who would describe themselves as introverts or extroverts.

**Famous introverts include Albert Einstein, Bill Gates, Emma Watson, Barack Obama, Meryl Streep, Steven Spielberg, and Mahatma Gandhi.**

**Famous extroverts include Oprah Winfrey, Ellen DeGeneres, Lady Gaga, Dwayne "The Rock" Johnson, Martin Luther King Jr., and Richard Branson.**

When we know and understand our tendencies, we can learn to develop the skills and tools we need to feel confident and comfortable in all kinds of social settings. This doesn't mean you're changing who you are to fit in; it just means that you might find that you can move in and out of certain types of personalities when needed.

Check out the lists in the appendices. It is not only helpful to have a better understanding of your own natural tendencies, but sometimes working to develop skills that don't come naturally can help to expand your comfort zones and make it easier to connect with different personalities of people.

# How Personality Shapes Interactions and Friendships

Think about your friend groups. Are you all introverts? Are you all extroverts? Do you have a fun mix of both? Personalities and friendships are just like our Fizeek: they have so many interesting characteristics, and they all look different. But the cool thing about that is it allows all these **different** **personalities** to help each other stretch and grow in ways we might not be able to if we went at it alone.

I have a lot of friends who challenge me to be better in certain ways; they highlight the really good parts of me, and I do the same for them. But there have been times in my life when I have formed relationships and connections with people who, instead of highlighting my best qualities, tested me and brought out some of my worst qualities. Once you have those bonds with people, it is hard to all of a sudden stop hanging out with them. But it happens. You meet people at school or in a group during your free time, and maybe they are part of the same after-school programs or extracurricular activities, so by default, you start doing things with them outside of that group. Makes total sense. You are just trying to form new relationships and be open to meeting new people.

This is where you have to go back to your core values and superpowers. Do these new people help you use those gifts? Do they acknowledge your strengths, or do they lead you down paths that force you outside the types of behaviors and choices that you feel truly reflect who you are—and the type of person that your parents and the people you love know you to be and God has created you to be? Do they encourage you to act contrary to your core values or strengthen those values?

If the answers aren't encouraging you to lean in to your unique Fizeek, then you have some tough choices to make. This would be a good conversation to have with your trusted adult about how to let connections go.

But if the answer is that they *are* encouraging you to lean in to your unique Fizeek, then you know you are with the right people.

# Diary of a Real Girl
## by Tate M..

I think that I am an **extrovert** around people I know because I am always very fun and silly! Sometimes in new situations with no one I know, I am very quiet and nervous. My friends usually don't see this side of me, so they often don't think I could ever be an **introvert**. I think that being this way is a good thing because I can always be happy, and I usually end up opening up in new situations.

# Chapter Challenge:
## Vision Boards for Future Selves

**Vision boards** help us do just that: envision and embrace our potential. They also help us understand that we are constantly growing and gaining new skills. So for this first activity, I want you to create a vision board for your future self, focusing on who you want to become, not just what you want to achieve. You can create a vision board several different ways, so pick the one that feels most empowering to you!

1. **Digital vision boards.** You can do it digitally in a Word document or use another creative program and use it to put images, graphics, words, or websites that inspire you or reflect the person you are striving to become.

2. **DIY vision boards.** If you like doing more hands-on art projects, you can get a poster board or foam board and draw or print out the images, designs, artworks, and words that depict that same vision for your future. The last option would be to get some markers or Post-it notes and put words, pictures, or quotes on your bathroom or bedroom wall or mirror to help you stay mindful and focused on those goals each day.

Then each week, you could pick a specific aspect of the vision board to be your "Focus of the Week." Decide and take one small step toward one of the visions on your board.

**vision board:** a collage of images and words representing a person's wishes or goals, intended to serve as inspiration or motivation.

# Chapter 12

# Walking Boldly—
# Be Uniquely YOU

*"For I know the plans I have for you," declares the Lord, "plans to prosper you and not to harm you, plans to give you hope and a future."*

*Jeremiah 29:11*

By the time Bella turned fourteen, she had learned to embrace everything that made her unique. **She walked the halls of her school with her head held high**, no longer afraid to share her ideas or try new things. She kept dancing, kept writing, and kept connecting with people through kindness and creativity.

Every night Bella would end her day with a prayer of gratitude.

"Thank You, God, for helping me find my superpowers and use them to make a difference," she would say.

One day as she stood by the bulletin board where her story was pinned, she overheard a younger student say, "I want to be like Bella when I'm older."

She had learned how to own her unique Fizeek, and now others were inspired to find theirs.

Bella smiled. So many more stories were in her future.

When I played soccer growing up, I was really fast, and I worked really hard to get better. I went to practices and camps and worked on my ball skills and fitness on my own. For several years, **I played on a team with a girl who was way better than me.** She was stronger and faster; she could take on anyone one-on-one. It was so frustrating because she was always late to practice—just late enough to miss the warm-up and the running. When we did drills, she usually came in last because she just didn't think they were important. It seemed like she just didn't need to try or just took her gifts for granted.

I always thought, *Man, if I just had a little bit of that talent, imagine what I could do with it. Why is she wasting it?*

By now you've learned that we all have different gifts that we're called to use and sharpen for the glory of God. And you yourself have already identified your superpowers (your gifts), how you can use them, and how you can make your gifts bigger and stronger. But we can also develop new ones with practice and attention.

If you have a true passion for something but maybe feel like you don't have the gifts to make an impact, don't let that be a barrier to you! Get involved anyway. You might play a different role in the group, or you might have to ask for extra help or support until you get the hang of it.

But God puts those little nudges in our heart for a reason, and He will keep nudging until we listen. So if you are feeling the pull to work on a specific project or join a new group at school, in your neighborhood, or at church, then just throw your hat in the ring—meaning, just jump in and see what happens! No one will ever be upset if you try, but if you don't try, then you will never know what could be possible.

God has called us to use our gifts in the service of others. This can look so many different ways. Even just **holding the door open** for someone who has their hands full at school or walking into the grocery store can be an act of service. Or it can be something way more involved like volunteering to join your school's community service club and spending your afternoons and free time serving the less fortunate or helping to raise money and awareness for certain causes.

One of the best ways to explore your superpowers is just to try them out in your day-to-day world. Let's say you think one of your superpowers is dancing. You love to dance, and you have a great ear for music and choreography. You have always loved creating routines and performing. There is a holiday fundraiser at your school, and they are asking for people to help out with the main event. You don't know what they need help with, but you think it is always nice to give back during the holidays when so many people are going without or don't have the things they need to stay warm, a nice meal, or any presents under the tree. So you sign up and find out that they are looking for entertainment for the big event at the end of the year. With a little planning and practice, you create a great dance for the event, get to share your gifts, and also end up helping in your unique Fizeek way!

*The only way to be deeply known,*
*is to allow yourself to be deeply seen.*
                                    *—Jennifer Dukes Lee*

# Exploring Outside Your Comfort Zone

Have you ever heard of a **comfort zone**? It's kinda like a safety net or a homebase. If you have ever played tag or capture the flag, it's like the zone where no one can get you or tag you out. You are protected and safe as long as you are in that space. When you are playing the game, and you feel danger coming, the other team attacking, your first thought is, *Where is the safety zone?*

In life we have those same zones. For many of us, this is at home or, even more specifically, in our bedroom. For others, maybe this is a neighbor's house or your grandparents' house. Perhaps you feel more at home at school, in your adviser's office, or in one of your teachers' rooms. We can go in, close the door, and know that nothing can hurt us or make us feel vulnerable.

Inside our comfort zone, we might let certain people in, the people we trust and can lean on when we need comfort or feel scared: parents or grandparents, aunts or uncles, siblings, teachers, coaches, even friends. In our comfort zone, we can be ourselves without fear of rejection or judgment. The types of activities we choose, the emotions we show, the stories we share—all these are easier in our comfort zone. It is normal and easy to want to stay there all the time. I mean, it makes sense. Why would anyone want to venture out and feel exposed at risk of being "tagged out," or maybe judged for showing those parts of ourselves that we usually only show in our safe space?

Well, here is the thing about comfort zones: they are small, they never change, and they don't challenge us or make us stronger because they allow us to just keep doing what we have always done. Doing what we have always done makes it hard to learn new things or have new experiences, meet new people, and try activities that can help us to spread our wings and find new superpowers! What if you have all these other, hidden, unexplored gifts, but you never unwrap them? What a total bummer that would be! I want to open *all* the gifts. There could be some supercool stuff in those uncomfortable soon-to-be-comfortable zones. (I say "soon-to-be-comfortable" zones because once you start growing and stretching and pushing the boundaries of your current comfort zones, they also grow and get bigger and bigger, so that no matter where you wander or how far you want to go, you feel brave, confident, and ready to face the opposition.)

Whenever you try something new, there is a chance you will stumble. Totally normal. If you are a **dancer**, and the choreographer adds a new step sequence, it takes a few rehearsals to get it. If you are an **actress** and the script gets rewritten or they change the timing of your cues, it's unlikely you will nail it on the first take. At basketball practice, the coach throws in a new last-second-shot play, and unless you are a WNBA star, you're probably not going to drain the three-pointer on the first try. Anything is possible, and you are pretty incredible, but you know what I mean. New things take some practice. But practice makes us better, and eventually, we get it.

A lot of people are afraid of failing. I used to be one of them. I thought if I messed up, it meant I wasn't good enough. I should be able to do it every time, all the time. Soon I realized that is just impossible. Failure is not something to be afraid of. In fact, there is no better feedback!

Every time you try something and it doesn't go the way you wanted, you learn something. You learn how to adjust, what you need to watch out for, or how you need to change your position, footwork, spacing. All those little nuggets of information come together, and then not only are you going to crush it, but you are probably going to do it even better because you were looking for all the information and potential challenges.

# Faith Over Fear

I went to school with the same group of girls (and boys) from kindergarten to eighth grade. In eighth grade, we had to choose a high school, and many of the girls from my class chose to go to the same all

girls high school as me. Although it felt like a new start in many ways (uniforms, new campus, different school colors and mascot), **I was still in school with all the same girls** who had been my friends since we were six years old. It was comfortable; it was familiar. They knew me better than anyone new at my school. Our parents were close, we knew each other's brothers and sisters, and we shared inside jokes.

As freshman year started, and we all got settled into new classes, sports, or other extracurricular activities, things suddenly felt different. **I was playing soccer, joined a travel team, and was gone most every weekend.** When I was in town, I had to catch up on school and spend time with my family. None of my girlfriends were athletes in high school; they chose other activities. They were in the drama club or on the student council. Some didn't do anything after school. They had time to shop, go to movies, have sleepovers, or go to the boys' school football games. I started to feel this wedge between us—not intentionally but just by nature of drifting in different directions. But I was afraid to try and find new friends. I didn't know if other people would accept me, open up their circles for me. They didn't know anything about me, and I didn't know them. It was scary, and I stayed stuck for a long time. I knew I hadn't found my people, but the people I knew were not the same anymore.

I let fear win—fear of rejection, fear of not measuring up, fear of hurting my group if I started hanging out with other people. And yet I knew something was missing. If I had been vulnerable, and if I had been willing to own my Fizeek and show up authentically, I might have had a much different high school experience. I might have found my people and built lasting and meaningful friendships if I had let faith, and not fear, direct my path. This can happen with friendships, or it can happen with your superpowers. If we allow fear to keep us stuck, not stepping out on faith and allowing others to see our authentic, awesome gifts, then we might never know how we can connect or impact those around us who don't know what we have to share.

When you have a gift for something, the world deserves to experience it through you. If you have **a voice that brings people to their feet**, if you have a heart that can lift others up from the darkest days, if you can **create art that makes others smile** or helps them to imagine the most beautiful, peaceful places, God calls us to make sure others get to experience those gifts. Those gifts are *superpower*-ful.

Have you ever been sitting in class having read the assignment, having completed all the reflection questions, and having studied, just in case there was a pop quiz? Then at the beginning of the discussion, your teacher throws out a really tough question. No one is answering, except you know the answer, but you are too afraid to raise your hand.

You think, *What if people think I am a know-it-all for answering? I don't want others to know that I did all this studying just to be prepared for class. What if I say the wrong thing? It will be safer not to answer.*

So you hold yourself back because of your fear, even though you spent all that time preparing for this specific situation. Since no one answered, the teacher hands out the pop quiz, and only later, you find out that if you'd just answered the questions when your teacher asked them, you wouldn't have had to take the pop quiz at all? Has that ever happened to you? How did it feel to let fear win?

What if it was like this instead: your teacher asks that same really tough question.

*Yes!* you think to yourself. *I knew she was going to ask that, and I studied really hard so I would be prepared when she did.*

So **you throw your hand up**, even though, again, no one else raises their hand. Of course, she calls on you. You answer the question with perfection. You are so proud of yourself for the hard work you put in on the reading assignment and the preparation. After you answer the question, your teacher announces that you will get to skip the pop quiz and everyone else will have to take it. The ultimate payoff. You feel bad that some of your classmates will have to take the quiz, but you did the work, and you put yourself out there  when no one else would. You were rewarded for using your knowledge and for the preparation you put into class that day.

Fear is one *big* reason people don't celebrate their talents. But fear is the opposite of faith. Did you ever think about it like that? It is impossible to trust God's plan for your life if you are afraid to step out and use the gifts He's given you. Faith is the ultimate trust that God's got you! It may not look the way you had imagined. It might come in the most unexpected and unplanned ways, but if we are afraid, then we will never try, and we will never be able to really experience the divine and amazing things that He has in store for us!

When we have found our superpowers, when we are fueling a healthy Fizeek, when we are keeping our body and brain strong, when we walk with purpose, celebrating our superpowers and sharing them with the world, is when we have fully developed our Fizeek. We are standing on a rock-solid foundation that allows us to stand up, step up, and show up. Because we have found our footing, we can confidently remain focused on our Divine purpose and share our superpowers with the world.

When we can be vulnerable, authentic, and step out of our comfort zones in the name of making a re-*mark*-able impact consistently with faith and not fear, then and only then do we truly own our unique Fizeek.

# Being Vulnerable and Authentic Lets Others Be Vulnerable and Authentic Too

Instead of a "Diary of a Real Girl" for this final chapter, I wanted to include a story from the book *The Happiness Dare* by Jennifer Dukes Lee:

Anna hosted a sleepover for several of her friends. One of the mothers informed me that her daughter would be bringing along her "lovie" and was worried that the other girls might tease her for sleeping with a ragged blanket—the same blanket that she'd slept with for ten years straight. It had moved with her from her crib to her toddler bed to her "big girl" bed. The blanket had taken long car rides with her, and it had soothed her when she felt lonely or hurt or afraid of the dark.

When this girl was around the people who knew her and loved her best, she was never afraid to bring the lovie into the light. But as she grew older, she began to keep it hidden from everyone else. She couldn't quite put a finger on the reason why. Why did something she loved so much feel like it had to be hidden? Somehow, the blanket had become a bit of a secret. Admitting that she slept with a lovie made this girl feel vulnerable and maybe a bit ashamed.

As night came, I dimmed the lights in the family room, where Anna and her friends would sleep. All the girls snuggled under blankets for a late-night movie. I pushed play on the remote. But that girl? She wanted her blanket. I could see how she was fighting a quiet battle on her insides.

This battle was about the risk of vulnerability. If she's like most of us, Anna's friend was asking herself the most paralyzing question in the universe: What will people think of me?

She made her choice. I watched as she walked to the bedroom, unzipped her bag, and quietly pawed through her belongings to find the love-worn blanket. From my seat in the family room, I saw what happened next.

The girl walked back into the room with her blanket tucked under her arm. One of the girls saw what she had retrieved from the bag. The girl had been found out.

"What's that?" asked the friend, pointing a finger at the lovie.

I was so proud of that little girl, because here's what she did next: She lifted her chin, mustered her voice, and took the first step toward an authentic relationship. She sat cross-legged on the couch and told her room of friends the truth. She told them how her mom's friend had made the blanket for her when she was a newborn, how it had traveled with her on a hundred car rides, how she once lost it at the park, and how it fell apart a few years ago so Grandma had to sew it back together. She showed everyone the long stitch mark, and it looked like a scar.

Everyone listened. No one laughed at her. No one judged. And then the most beautiful thing happened. One by one, each of the girls pushed back the covers, walked into the bedroom, and unzipped her own duffel bag. Out came the ragged blankets, a bear with a missing eye, a plush doll. Every girl in the room was hiding a secret lovie in her bag.

That was the Night of the Great Unzipping.

Each girl dragged her own lovie into the living room, and then they took turns telling their stories—about lovies loved, lovies lost, and lovies found again.

Everyone slept better that night. Because someone had the guts to go first.[5]

Throughout this chapter, we've talked about having faith over fear in order to share our gifts with others so that God's light can shine on them through us. When we do that, when we choose to act in spite of our fear, we're also choosing to be vulnerable. We don't know how other people may respond to us, but we're doing it anyway. Just as using our gifts allows and encourages others to use their gifts, being vulnerable allows others to be vulnerable too.

The girls in the story all wanted to bring out their lovies, but they were scared of how the others would respond. It wasn't until one girl had the faith and courage to be vulnerable about her fears and needs that the others felt safe enough to do the same. The next time you're scared to be vulnerable or be authentically you, instead of sinking into yourself because of the fear, instead of feeling isolated in it, think about the girl sitting next to you, who might need you to take courage and be vulnerable so that she can be vulnerable too.

Before you close this book to go out and share your superpowers with the world, I wanted to leave you with a song. It's by an artist named Megan Woods from her 2024 album, *The Truth*. The song is also called, "The Truth:"

> ***The truth is I am my Father's child /***
> ***I make Him proud and I make Him smile /***
> ***I was made in the image of a perfect King /***
> ***He looks at me and wouldn't change a thing /***
> ***The truth is I am truly loved /***
> ***By a God who's good when I'm not good enough /***
> ***I don't belong to the lies, I belong to You.***

Check Out the
Song Here

Now you go stand up, step up, and show up in God's way, every day!

# A NOTE FOR THE OLD FOLKS
## (That's Your Parents)

If you are reading this, then my guess is you bought my book for your daughter, niece, or any important girl in your life (or you are considering it). You will not be disappointed! And I promise I will guide and support her as she explores her dreams and navigates the challenges that girls go through growing up. I wanted to share with you a little about me so you know who is talking to your girl.

I grew up in Nashville, the daughter of two incredible parents—supportive, driven models of love and integrity. They are still married today, more than fifty years later, and still as in love as ever. I grew up in a Christian home, church on Sunday mornings and nights, youth group on Wednesdays. My parents taught Sunday school, and many of our friends were from church.

As I got into late middle school, I became very focused on sports: club soccer, AAU basketball, travel softball teams. Every season was another commitment. We started traveling most weekends, and life changed; priorities shifted. Our faith was still important, but the time we spent on it became overshadowed by activities. We found other ways to practice our faith, but it just started to look different. I think this happens to many families as kids get more involved in extracurriculars and find new passions. We want to let them explore those, and I think we should.

Anyway, my love of sports continued into high school and even into my early college years, but a back injury at eighteen changed the trajectory of my athletic future. Now sitting on the sidelines, I found myself lost. So much of my identity, how I defined myself, and how others always saw me was gone. I was just Tiff. And I wasn't sure who that was.

My drive, my hunger for competition—the need to achieve and impress—began to take root as a pretty nasty eating disorder. I struggled with control. I was, and still very much am, a perfectionist. All the things that had served me well as an athlete like discipline, structure, and a desire to achieve higher levels of performance turned into something else. They became compulsive exercise and hyperfocusing on what I ate and how much. All this was self-imposed. I never battled childhood weight issues. My parents never talked about dieting, nor did they model negative body image behaviors.

My struggles, I believe, were the result of this loss of identity and not seeing the value in who I was but rather only what I was able to do. When the "what I did" (competitive sports) was gone, I looked for other ways to compete and to find structure in my world. My body became the training ground.

This battle went on for many years, until I began to study the science of the body and the brain: nutrition, exercise science, and sports psychology. I started to learn how they are intimately related—how what we feed our body can impact how we think, how we feel, and how we effectively deal with life's challenges. Fuel is the energy we use to chase our goals and build our dreams, along with the power of the mind—using our thoughts to support our passions and build self-belief rather than self-doubt. To see the things we are capable of rather than what is standing in our way.

More than the body and the brain, though, I also began to rebuild my relationship with God. I started to dive into scripture, to remind myself that I am *His* perfectly imperfect creation. He knit me together exactly as I was meant to be, and when I began trying to manipulate that with my choices, I was dishonoring His divine design. Faith became the foundation that helped me reestablish my purpose and passion and find my strength again, both physically and mentally.

I could not have done this without support, coaching, and the people who believed in me. I built a life team that encouraged me to find my superpowers again. The gifts that had always been there but had gotten lost in the pursuit of perfection.

Now I get to be that coach, that team captain, for clients every day. Today I run a private performance nutrition practice. I coach clients, both youth and adults, on the benefits of fueling their body for peak performance. Early in my career, I worked with competitive athletes on mental resilience programs, helping them to battle things like self-doubt, performance anxiety, or negative self-talk. I know what it is like to be your own worst critic. I know what it feels like to attach so much of your identity to the activities you do well—or the ones you just love so much they become part of who you are. I know what it is like to fight the inner voice that wants to push you, sometimes beyond what is necessary or healthy.

Here's the thing: I would never trade in my struggles. I gained insurmountable strength in those struggles. And most importantly, they have allowed me to write this book. To understand the vital areas of development and potential pitfalls that we can all fall victim to as we grow into our best selves. My hope is that through these pages, and the chapter challenges, our girls will learn to stand up, step up, and show up with the skills they need to leap over barriers and into the life they were meant to live.

## What's Your Role?

As always, be their biggest cheerleader. Be the unshakable voice of support and guidance while allowing them to try and falter. We cannot insulate our kiddos from failure, but we can help them to recognize that failure isn't fatal—it is feedback. The lessons we learn through successes are priceless. But the lessons learned through setbacks are the ones that are going to motivate us to grow, adjust, and push through those barriers that are holding us back.

Help your girls be their own advocates. Teach them to communicate what they need and to ask for help. Needing support is not a weakness—in fact, it is a sign of ultimate strength, a strength of character in knowing that we don't always know. And more importantly, teach them that with God on their side, and you in their corner, they are never, ever alone.

Just like I mentioned in the introduction to the girls, I am here to be a resource and a safe place. If you ever need a place to drop your thoughts or are seeking additional support for yourself or your daughters, I am just on the other side of an email. I hope you and your girls enjoy reading this book as much as I have enjoyed writing it.

Dr. Tiff

# Appendix 1
# **Additional Resources**

When writing this book, I wanted to include a list of additional resources for parents or caregivers. This is a tough age to navigate, and we all need help in one way or another at some point. The following is a list of organizations I recommend to my in-person clients that you and your girl(s) may also find useful.

## **Superpower Support**

Strength Finder Assessment

https://www.gallup.com/cliftonstrengths/en/250430/strengths-based-tweens-creating-empowered-adolescence.aspx

Lifeway Young Adults Spiritual Gifts Survey

https://youngadults.lifeway.com/2010/06/spiritual-gifts-survey/

## **Sports Resources**

Positive Coaching Alliance

https://positivecoach.org/

Youth Sport Psychology

https://www.youthsportspsychology.com/youth_sports_psychology_blog/

# Information and Support for Eating Disorders

National Eating Disorders Association:
https://www.nationaleatingdisorders.org/


Book Recommendation: 8 Keys to Recovery from an Eating Disorder

https://a.co/d/fA754Oo

# Substance Use and Mental Health Resources

SAMHSA

https://www.samhsa.gov/


National Alliance on Mental Illness (NAMI)

https://www.nami.org/your-journey/kids-teens-and-young-adults/

# Additional Activities for Chapter 4

Continuing with the list of specific ideas for sharpening your superpowers, here are some additional activities you may be interested in trying:

## STEM (Science, Technology, Engineering, and Math) Activities

- **Coding and Robotics:** Dive into the world of technology by creating animations, games, and robots with platforms like Scratch, LEGO Mindstorms, or Code.org. These activities make problem-solving and logical thinking exciting and fun.

- **Science Experiments:** Get hands-on with fun experiments like building volcanoes, making slime, or testing chemical reactions. Science comes to life when you can see, touch, and create!

- **Engineering Challenges:** Build bridges, design simple machines, and experiment with DIY engineering kits. These activities spark creativity, critical thinking, and a love for innovation

## Creative Arts and Crafts

- **Painting and Drawing:** Express yourself through art using watercolors, acrylics, or even digital tools. Create pieces that reflect your imagination and emotions.

- **Craft Projects:** Design and create jewelry, knit a scarf, or sew your own designs. Hands-on crafting brings ideas to life and results in unique, beautiful pieces.

- **Photography:** Capture the world through your lens! Learn the basics of photography, and discover how to tell stories through pictures.

- **DIY Projects:** Get creative with Pinterest-inspired crafts, or upcycle household items into something new and exciting.

## Performing Arts

- **Drama and Theater:** Step into the spotlight by acting in plays or joining a drama club. Build confidence, improve public speaking, and bring stories to life.

- **Dance:** Whether it's ballet, hip-hop, or contemporary, dancing is a fun way to stay active, express yourself, and connect with music.

- **Music Lessons:** Learn to play an instrument or join a choir to develop musical skills, boost confidence, and explore your passion for sound.

## Sports and Physical Activities

- **Team Sports:** Play soccer, basketball, volleyball, or softball to build teamwork, improve coordination, and have fun while staying active.

- **Individual Sports:** Try swimming, tennis, gymnastics, or martial arts to challenge yourself, develop discipline, and celebrate personal achievements.

- **Yoga and Mindfulness:** Practice beginner yoga or mindfulness exercises to improve focus, relax, and connect with yourself.

## Writing and Storytelling

- **Creative Writing:** Bring your imagination to life through journaling, writing short stories, or even starting a blog. Writing is a powerful way to express your thoughts and ideas.

- **Poetry:** Experiment with words and emotions by writing poetry or performing spoken word. Poetry is a great way to share your voice and creativity.

- **Book Clubs:** Read and discuss books with friends to explore new ideas, share perspectives, and build a love for literature.

## Community Service and Leadership

- **Volunteering:** Make a difference by helping at animal shelters, environmental projects, or community centers. Giving back feels good and teaches valuable life lessons.

- **Girl Scouts and Leadership Clubs:** Join groups like Girl Scouts or student council to develop leadership skills, teamwork, and confidence.

## Outdoor Adventures

- **Hiking and Nature Exploration:** Explore the outdoors, go birdwatching, or learn survival skills while developing a deep appreciation for nature.

- **Camping and Stargazing:** Set up a tent in your backyard or go on a camping trip to experience adventure and connect with the night sky.

## Culinary Arts

- **Baking and Cooking:** Learn to make simple dishes or bake delicious treats like cookies and cupcakes. Cooking is both a creative and practical skill.

- **Culinary Classes:** Take beginner cooking classes to explore different cuisines and develop new techniques in the kitchen.

## Entrepreneurship

- **Starting a Small Business:** Turn creativity into a business by making and selling crafts, baked goods, or handmade jewelry while learning valuable business skills.

- **DIY Fundraisers:** Organize a fundraiser or sell handmade items for a cause you care about, gaining leadership experience and making a difference.

## Cultural Exploration

- **Language Learning:** Pick up a new language using fun apps like Duolingo, or join a language club to expand your communication skills.

- **Exploring Different Cultures:** Discover new traditions, try international recipes, or attend cultural festivals to broaden your understanding of the world.

## Tech-Free and Relaxing Hobbies

- **Board Games and Puzzles:** Strengthen your critical thinking and problem-solving skills while having fun with friends and family.

- **Mindfulness Activities:** Take time to relax with activities like coloring, meditation, or simple breathing exercises that help with focus and self-care.

## Gardening and Nature Projects

- **Starting a Garden:** Grow your own vegetables, flowers, or houseplants to learn patience, responsibility, and the joy of caring for nature.
- **Sustainable Living Projects:** Explore eco-friendly activities like composting or creating a pollinator garden to make a positive impact on the environment.

# Appendix 3

# Additional Skill Development Activities for Chapter 11

Below are lists for developing introversion or extroversion skills:

## Ideas for Developing Introversion Skills

- Create a quiet retreat: A dedicated space at home where you can recharge and engage in solitary activities like reading, drawing, or quiet reflection.

- Encourage hobbies and creative outlets: Finding structured groups that have shared interests can provide opportunities to explore passions. This will develop skills and boost self-esteem.

- Foster one-on-one connections: Develop meaningful friendships through smaller, more intimate settings. Playdates, shared interests, and activities with a few close friends can help build strong connections.

- Teach self-care practices: Activities like journaling, mindfulness, and physical exercise can promote well-being and provide opportunities to explore interests.

- Advocate for their needs: Be your own advocate in social situations. Maybe even talking to the host ahead of time. "It would really help if I could meet everyone first or if everyone could introduce themselves in a small setting," or "If it's okay, maybe I could bring some games or puzzles to share with everyone." This is a way to communicate boundaries and provide reassurance and guidance when needed.

# Ideas for Developing Extroversion Skills

- Provide social opportunities: Engage in group activities, sports, and community events where you can meet new people and build social skills.

- Teach safety and awareness: It is important to remember the potential dangers of being so friendly and outgoing! Although you have heard it since you were little, talking to strangers or sharing personal information online can be dangerous.

- Encourage active listening: it is important to learn social skills like listening to others and respecting their perspectives. These skills enhance communication abilities and foster meaningful connections.

- Promote downtime and reflection: Help your child find a balance between social interactions and quiet moments. Encourage them to engage in activities like reading, writing, or solitary hobbies that allow them to recharge.

- Embrace their enthusiasm: Celebrate your child's outgoing nature and support their passions. Encourage them to explore new activities, nurture their curiosity, and express themselves freely.

# Glossary of Terms

| Word | Definition | Page Number |
|------|-----------|-------------|
| Beliefs | Trust, faith, or confidence in someone or something. | 32 |
| Carbohydrate | Carbohydrates (or carbs) are the sugars, starches, and dietary fibers that occur in certain foods. The body breaks them down into glucose, which provides energy for bodily functions. | 56 |
| Confidence | A feeling of self-assurance arising from one's appreciation of one's own abilities or qualities. | 114 |
| Empathy | The ability to understand and share the feelings of another. | 134 |
| Enzyme | A biological catalyst that is almost always a protein. It speeds up the rate of a specific chemical reaction in the cell. The enzyme is not destroyed during the reaction and is used over and over. | 61 |

# Glossary of Terms

| Word | Definition | Page Number |
|------|-----------|-------------|
| Extroversion | A personality trait or style characterized by a preference for or orientation to engaging socially with others. | 147 |
| Fats | Nutrients in food that the body uses to build cell membranes, nerve tissue (including the brain), and hormones. The body also uses fat as fuel. | 62 |
| Introversion | A personality trait or style characterized by a preference for or orientation to one's own thoughts and feelings. | 148 |
| Mission Statement | A formal summary of the aims and values of a company, organization, or individual. | 40 |
| Nutrition | The process of providing or obtaining the food necessary for health and growth. | 54 |

# Glossary of Terms

| Word | Definition | Page Number |
|------|-----------|-------------|
| Pep Talk | A talk intended to make someone feel more courageous or enthusiastic. | 123 |
| Physique | The form, size, and development of a person's body. | 10, 97 |
| Protein | Any of various naturally occurring extremely complex substances that consist of amino-acid residues joined by peptide bonds. | 60 |
| Values | A person's principles or standards of behavior; one's judgment of what is important in life. | 32 |
| Vision Board | A collage of images and words representing a person's wishes or goals, intended to serve as inspiration or motivation. | 154 |

# Biographies of
# Diary Contributors

## Chapter 2

**Emma W.**

Hi! My name is Emma. I am 10 years old, in 5th grade, and live in Nashville, TN. I have two sisters and I am the (middle) child. I love spending my free time dancing and reading.

My biggest dream right now is to become a better dancer and be Clara in *The Nutcracker*.

- Favorite Movie: *Wicked*
- Favorite Song & Artist: "Speak Now" by Taylor Swift
- Favorite Dessert: Anything caramel
- Favorite Part of My Unique FIZEEK!: My eyes

## Chapter 3

**Skyler R.**

Hi! My name is Skyler R. I am 12 years old, in 6th grade, and live in Nashville, TN. I have one brother and I am the oldest child.

I love spending my free time hanging out with friends and family, dancing, and playing outside. My biggest dream right now is to be in a TV show or movie.

- Favorite Song & Artist: "I'm So Blessed" & Sabrina Carpenter
- Favorite Dessert: Peppermint ice cream cake
- Favorite Part of My Unique FIZEEK!: My eyes

# Chapter 4

### Sophia B.

 Hi, my name is Sophia B. I am 13 years old and I'm in 8th grade and I live in Grand Ledge, Michigan. I have one sister and I'm the youngest. I love spending my free time hanging out with friends. My biggest dream is to become a teacher.

- My Favorite Movie: *Twisters*
- My Favorite Artist: Daniel Caesar
- My Favorite Dessert: Vanilla cake
- My Favorite Part of My Unique FIZEEK!: My freckles

### Hanna T.

 Hi! My name is Hanna T. I am 43 years old, and I live in Westminster, MA. I have one brother and one sister. I am the youngest child. I love spending my free time outside, with my family and playing piano. My biggest dream right now is to travel and record music.

- Favorite Movie: *August Rush*
- Favorite Song & Artist: Hans Zimmer & *Dune* soundtrack
- Favorite Dessert: Homemade apple pie
- Favorite Part of My Unique FIZEEK!: Being authentic and trying new things

# Chapter 5

### Izzy C.

Hi! My name is Isabel C. I am 16 years old, I am in 11th grade, and I live in Franklin, TN. I am an only child. I love spending my free time with my friends making funny videos. My biggest dream right now is to figure skate for Team USA. I hope to skate at Nationals in the next few years.

- Favorite Movie: *Ready Player One*
- Favorite Song & Artist: "Water" & SZA
- Dessert: Chocolate chip cookies
- Favorite Part of My Unique FIZEEK!: How muscular I am

# Chapter 6

### Charlotte B.

Hi! My name is Charlotte B. I'm 12 years old, in 6th grade, and live in Brentwood, Tennessee. I have two younger sisters and I'm the oldest child. I love spending my free time playing my cello, baking, and playing tennis. My biggest dream right now is to get good at cello.

- Some Fun Facts about Me: I can play cello, I can bake, I have two guinea pigs and a dog, and I have had frogs before.
- Favorite Song & Artist: Anything pop, country or orchestral!
- Favorite Dessert: Key lime pie
- Favorite Part of My Unique FIZEEK!: I am tall

# Chapter 7

### Karsen H.

 Hi! My name is Karsen H. I am 13 years old, in 7th grade, and live in Holly Springs, NC. I have one brother and I am the youngest child. I love spending my free time doing anything active and being outside. My biggest dream right now is to win the Cheerleading Worlds.

- Favorite Movie: *Moana*
- Favorite Song & Artist: "You Should Probably Leave" & Chris Stapleton
- Favorite Dessert: Brownies
- Favorite Part of My Unique FIZEEK!: Being active and proud of who I am.

# Chapter 8

### Macy W.

 Hi! My name is Macy W. I'm 13 years old, in 8th grade, and live in Omaha, Nebraska. I have a twin brother and a little sister. I love spending my free time reading. My biggest dream right now is to win at the Nebraska State Horse Show in showmanship, horsemanship, and barrel racing.

- Some Fun Facts about Me: I love baking when I'm bored. I make the world's best cookies according to my stepdad! I've ridden horses my whole life. I have two horses of my own: Carol, my show horse, and Sugar, my speed racing horse.
- Favorite Movie: *Perks of Being a Wallflower*
- Favorite Song & Artist: "Do Not Wait" & Taylor Swift
- Favorite Dessert: Ice cream
- Favorite Part of My Unique Fizeek: How I can help empower girls with their self-confidence

# Chapter 9

### Mackenzie

Hi! My name is Mackenzie. I am 14 years old, in 9th grade, and live in Nashville, TN. I have two sisters and I am the oldest child.

I love spending my free time doing ballet, hanging with my friends and organizing. My biggest dream right now is to go to college and be on their dance team.

- Favorite Movie: *How to Lose a Guy in 10 Days*
- Favorite Song & Artist: "Night Changes" & Benson Boone
- Favorite Dessert: Chocolate-covered strawberries
- Favorite Part of My Unique FIZEEK!: My hair

# Chapter 10

### Lauren W.

Hi! My name is Lauren W. I am 14 years old and currently in 9th grade. I live in Nashville, TN. I have one brother, and I am the oldest. I love spending my free time horseback riding. My biggest dream right now is to complete mission trips and continue volunteering at the Nashville Zoo.

- Some Fun Facts about Me: I've been riding horses since I was six. I'm a lefty, and even though I have dyslexia, I love to write.
- Favorite Movie: *The Hobbit*
- Favorite Song & Artist: "Come Alive" & Lauren Daigle
- Favorite Dessert: Cheesecake!
- Favorite Part of My Unique FIZEEK!: My sense of humor

### Keller B.

Hi! My name is Keller B. I am 11 years old, in 6th grade, and live in Atlanta, Georgia. I have one sister and I am the youngest child. I love spending my free time playing sports and watching TV. My biggest dream right now is to pitch at 55 miles per hour.

- Favorite Movie: *Interstellar*
- Favorite Song & Artist: "Open Arms" & SZA
- Favorite Dessert: Jeni's ice cream
- Favorite Part of My Unique FIZEEK!: My body is fully healthy

## Chapter 11

### Tate M.

Hi! My name is Tate M. I am 15 years old, in 9th grade, and live in Nashville, Tennessee. I have one sister and I am the youngest child. I love spending my free time with my friends. My biggest dream right now is to travel more.

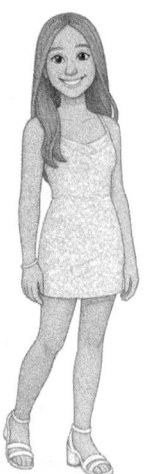

- My Favorite TV Show: *Gossip Girl*
- My Favorite Singer: Sabrina Carpenter
- My Favorite Dessert: Frozen yogurt
- My Favorite Part of My Unique FIZEEK!: My blue eyes

# References

## Chapter 10

[1] "Big Kindness: Stories to Inspire Compassion," SIYLI, June 5, 2024, https://siyli.org/resources/blog/big-kindness-stories-to-inspire-compassion#:~:text=When%20Dylan%20Siegel%20was%20in%20first%20grade%2C,and%20got%20his%20school%20to%20make%20copies.

[2] All Our Kids, https://aokarts.org/

[3] "15 Stories of Kindness to Brighten Your Day." Smiley Movement. Accessed February 13, 2025. https://smileymovement.org/news/random-acts-of-kindness.

## Chapter 11

[4] Van den Akker, Alithe L., Daniel A. Briley, Andrew D. Grotzinger, Jennifer L. Tackett, Elliot M. Tucker-Drob, and K. Paige Harden, "Adolescent Big Five Personality and Pubertal Development: Pubertal Hormone Concentrations and Self-Reported Pubertal Status," Developmental Psychology 57, no. 1 (January 2021): 60–72, https://doi.org/10.1037/dev0001135.

## Chapter 12

[5] Jennifer Dukes Lee, The Happiness Dare: Pursuing Your Hearts Deepest, Holiest, and Most Vulnerable Desire (Tyndale Momentum, 2016), 105–107.

www.ingramcontent.com/pod-product-compliance
Lightning Source LLC
Chambersburg PA
CBHW071354120626
46546CB00002B/679